T

A to ZEN

of

TRAVEL

Sarah Tucker

Published by New Generation Publishing in 2014

Copyright © Sarah Tucker 2014

First Edition

www.newgeneration-publishing.com

 New Generation **Publishing**

DEDICATION

Always for Tom
May all your journeys be blessed

FOREWORD

by Professor Edward de Bono

As with most travel books, the author has done a great deal of traveling. But what is different from most travel books is that this book is about 'thinking about travel'. Sarah Tucker has used from time to time my thinking tools, like the attention-directing PMI.

Imagine that you are in an art gallery looking at a painting you like very much. Suddenly one of the staff comes along and tells you all about the painting: what to notice, what to look at, about the artist etc. The attractiveness of the painting increases very considerably. Sometimes.

Imagine that you have left your spectacles somewhere and are looking at a map. Everything is blurred and confused. Someone hands you your spectacles and your vision improves dramatically. But it is up to you if what you interpret you see as more attractive. So it is that some will find, for example, Canada, incredibly beautiful and others not so.

Sarah Tucker writes about destinations and journeys but from a refreshing perspective. How we perceive a place is swayed by how we define it. Sarah identifies why some destinations and journeys are more emotionally fulfilling than others and why the emotional process of moving on correlates with the literal journey – but only if you take the right path.

The thinking Sarah encourages is not the thinking that you have to do before and during an exam. It is more like the thinking you do as you appreciate a fine wine and notice all the different aspects of the taste. The perception and reaction is purely your own. How you choose to share it with others, articulate it, is secondary. It doesn't make the experience of it any less real to you.

It is all about perception and the emotion you take with it at the time of your journey. Since perception is by far the most important part of thinking, where you direct attention is very important.

This innovative, fascinating book will greatly increase your enjoyment of travel – how you think about it, how you experience it, and how the experience of travel enhances you for different reasons in different ways. It is a book you should read, just as if you use glasses you should always have them with you to improve your sight. Thinking improves your sight – and so your appreciation and enjoyment.

Professor Edward de Bono

WHAT THE BOOK IS ABOUT

Twenty years from now, you will be more disappointed by the things you didn't do than by the ones you did do. So throw off the bowlines. Sail away from the safe harbour. Catch the trade winds in your sails. Explore. Dream. Discover.

Mark Twain

Journeys never lead you to where you expect. This guidebook tells you how to look at things rather than what to look at and how journeys will and do help you emotionally – if you let them. As you will learn some cultures are innately more comfortable with expressing their emotion than the English. This allows them to accept and move on from their anger, grief, heartbreak, depression, loneliness, whatever, more easily. So it follows, when we are in their country and immersed in their culture and customs we will assimilate and assume some of them for ourselves. This may take us on an emotional journey that will have a far more enduring and positive effect than a tan. And it is as relevant if not more so for men than it is for women. The book 'Eat, Pray, Love' brilliant though it is, is possibly aimed at an almost exclusively female market. I asked Professor De Bono to work with me on A to Zen, because I wanted this book to be relevant to both genders, and for all ages. And from my research, men need emotional release even more than women do.

Of course, not all journeys help emotionally. Travel to a culture that is even more anally retentive than our own (and there are some) and the reverse may happen. But it also depends whom you travel with and how you travel.

And are cultural stereotypes for real? Are the Chinese better at dealing with grief than we are? Do they sob and go to counseling or is it something they accept and move on from rather than dwell as the western world appears to do?

Are the French much better at standing up for themselves? And saying no?

Are the Italians better at dealing with heartbreak than the British?

Are South Americans more passionate than us?

From my travels I have noticed cultures are defined by their history, their language, food, dress, but also by the distinct way they react to emotion. Their own emotion and how they react to emotion in others. I asked Dr Rachel Andrews, clinical psychologist about her view on the impact of travel and how new cultures impact on psychological development.

I worked with her on my book HAVE TEENAGER WILL TRAVEL, which was initially destined to be a definitive guidebook on where to go and what to do with hard to please teenagers.

However, I quickly realized – following interviewing thousands of teenagers and their parents about their travels – the issue wasn't the specifics of where to go and what to see, but that travel essentially makes the teenager 'tick'. Furthermore, it was less to do with where they visited, and what they did when there, but more to do with the type of person they were and also how they traveled.

I learnt that the psychological impact of travel on teenagers is significant. Travel in all its forms, be it a weekend city break or a trek round Thailand, greatly helps with self-esteem, sense of self, confidence, sociability, ability to communicate and adapt, and overall level of compassion. They met role models they considered 'real'. As one fifteen year old told me, 'The Beckhams are not good enough. The role models I met on my holiday were real."

But does this apply to adults who may be more set in their ways and carry considerably more emotional baggage than their teenage counterparts?

"Yes," says Dr Rachel Andrews, "The English as a culture tend to be embarrassed seeing emotion in others. It is true, we view outbursts of raw emotion on TV, in soap operas, in reality TV shows, but we accept these emotions because we subliminally know they are not real. We may even accept emotional outburst with friends and family, but in general, showing your emotions, your grief, anger, sadness, depression, loneliness is still considered a very unhealthy and unsociable thing to do. We literally box up our emotions over the years, in denial about their existence until the box is so full it bursts. Our inability to release and deal with emotion has physical implications as well as psychological ones.

"Stress, for example, is now considered to be a trigger for cancer – or rather our inability to deal with stress is a trigger for cancer. If we do not open the box of suppressed emotion it will at some point burst. This usually happens in the mid forties (the mid life crisis) but can happen at any time – it just depends when the box starts to over flow and the amount of emotion you have stored over time. It is then you get the emotional tsunami or breakdown, wondering where it came from when it has been there all along, waiting to be released.

"We are innately reticent in our own country but when we travel we tend to literally 'come out of ourselves' because we introduce ourselves to cultures that are more open and accepting. No wonder many of us find solace by traveling, not just because we may be doing and seeing something new, but because we have left the restrictive culture behind. We feel more at ease to express our emotions within cultures that are happy to express theirs – cultures that do not judge you in the same way we feel judged in the UK. Even if we don't go to a more relaxed culture emotionally, just by being away from those around us at home who may judge us is also a form of emotional release.

"Saying the Germans are brusque, the English are anally retentive emotionally, the French have high self esteem and the Italians are passionate are playing to over generalized stereotypes. But each stereotype was borne from observation so somewhere there is truism amongst these descriptions. In reality, you find all these 'types' in every nation, but there are cultures where attitude toward children in particular shows an empathy and compassion other cultures lack. Indeed how we react to children and animals is telling of how we react to our own vulnerabilities and our own emotions.

The compassion we show to the vulnerable and the vulnerability in others is merely a reflection of the compassion we show to the vulnerability in ourselves.

We are prone to opening up more when we are in an environment where we feel able to."

But it is not just our experiences that shape us. We are more than the sum of our experiences. When we develop our thinking, this is what happens. Professor Edward de Bono, who kindly wrote the Foreword, taught me this. We see with better eyes, we think more clearly, creatively, or to use the word the Professor introduced to the global English language, 'laterally'. So I decided to use the Professor's thinking tools to delve more deeply into the world of travel.

His journey, he tells me, was borne from being a physician and a psychologist – his right and left brain both being used to explore and explain thinking. The process of thought. Having attention to detail but seeing the bigger picture, the impact of emotions, the subconscious, and knowing there's more out there than meets the eye, literally and metaphorically.

The Professor gave the world a set of tools to think deeper, more creatively and brilliantly. And the world accepted it. How phenomenal is that?

He asked me as his guest for the weekend. I sat and asked him questions, stopping briefly so he could eat and drink and breathe, and listened to him. This man was the ultimate motivational speaker in the 80s, and he still is. Life takes you on interesting journeys if you have courage and charm, if you think laterally and stay open to what is around you. On all my travels I do this instinctively, but most do not.

I didn't know the Professor was in the room that evening. I didn't expect to meet him, and I didn't expect to have the courage to go up to him and say hello. This book is not about making the most of your journeys; it is about your journeys making the most of you.

Thank you, Professor, for making that journey on 31st December 2013 so worthwhile.

ONE: THE TYPES OF JOURNEY WE TAKE

Don't tell me how educated you are, tell me how much you have traveled
Mohammed the Prophet

You don't have to learn something new on each journey taken, but something new about yourself would be a start.

Dance journeys –

Those journeys which match our mood at the moment. Stressed – beach or spa. Wanting to invigorate – trekking Kilimanjaro, then beach holiday on the coast. Best when taken alone or someone you know you are on the same wave-length with, as everyone literally goes at their own pace in their own time. Some want the passion and pace of the tango, others want the dignity and rigid timing of the waltz, others want to go with their own thing – the American smooth. Just watch Strictly Come Dancing and see what it would look like if a partner did tango while you tried the foxtrot. You get the idea.

Ego trips – it's all about you

Those journeys where it's not about the destination, it's all about you – conquering, traveling, tick-boxing. Mountain climbing, trips to Antarctica, Route 66 on a Harley Davidson. That sort of thing, usually taken by middle-aged men with self identity and esteem issues. Not always men, but usually men. The journey rarely satiates their appetite for self-appraisement.

Elephant journeys – bite size chunks

Typically round the world, and bitten off in 'bite size chunks'. They are also called 'elephant journeys' because elephants allegedly never forget and these journeys are about wanting to forget. Round the world trips tend to end early because you either a) find someone you love en route b) fall out of love with the person you are with en route c) decide to stay somewhere longer than the schedule/budget allows. These can also be smaller journeys but which are big for you – as in emotionally. Returning to a place you went with a past lover and seeing if you feel the same about a) the relationship b) the place. This is a big step to take emotionally even if not physically. Best taken spontaneously. Too much thought and you won't go.

Groundhog Holidays

Risk averse holidays: returning to the same destination. Taking exactly the same path each year due to needing to know what is coming, wanting to relax into the break more quickly, and wanting to have as much control as possible over your enjoyment and expectations. Nothing new is learnt until a different journey or destination is eventually chosen.

Dung beetle journeys – eat, shit and die

Sounds horrible, doesn't it, but a lot of us go on these sort of journeys. Usually as children when we don't want to go somewhere but the parents are paying. We do not want to be there. Ironically there are a lot of adults also in the same situation who are with someone they don't love, like, or respect. This becomes blatantly transparent if you are with someone on a romantic break and aren't in love with them any more. Often couples go to romantic destinations to rekindle romance, but it frequently makes it clear there's nothing left. That said, dung beetles are a very important part of the process. They clear up the mess and these type of journeys teach lessons which otherwise we would avoid or deny. And you may be surprised. There may be something worth fighting for.

Envelope journeys – don't know what is coming next

Exciting journeys when you are spontaneous about the next destination or stop and go where the opportunity leads you. I once interviewed Tara Palmer-Tomkinson who told me she and Tamara Beckwith would go to the airport and throw a dice on which destination they would go to next. She always said she would go wherever it took her. Nice if you have the time and the money. But a little uninspired.

Room 171 journeys – where you decide what good looks like, despite what you are told

There is a room in the Uffizi in Florence, where there are wonderful paintings. They are not by famous painters – as in Botticelli and Da Vinci – but by lesser known artists. And every time I go there, they are in a different room (they move the paintings about a lot). But I still like the same ones. I can't be fooled into thinking that just because someone tells me a piece of art is better than the next, it must be true. This is the type of journey you take despite what the media, your friends, your family, your neighbours say. It is one you know is right for you, at the time. You can't even say why it is, you just know it is.

Red Box journeys – so named after the Prime Minister's Red Box of must-signs and must-look-ats every day.

This journey is a journey where you have an intrinsic need to accomplish something. Paint, scuba dive, and come back with some type of completion. It is not about tick-boxing. It is a journey where you feel an internal sense of accomplishment and something that has to be done. For example, scattering a relative's ashes.

Heartbreak journeys – healing the heart

Journeys taken to forget loved ones, or a lost love. Heartbreak journeys focus on acceptance and that old chestnut 'moving on'. Easy to say, bloody difficult to do. Please note, healing the heart is not the same as toughening it. The best places to heal the heart and journeys are those where you fall in love with yourself. Not the idea of you being with someone else, but by being you. Ironically not desert islands because that is not the real world. Nor places like Ibiza where everyone is high on life but not quite sure what life is. Florence is good, Venice is not, Malta is good, Maldives is not, Queenstown is good, Queensland is not. Heartbreak journeys are usually situated in wilderness although for the young, they choose anywhere the night-life is active although this invariably fails to heal the heart, merely toughens it. Manufactured romance or fun is not the same as the real thing. Bit like love really.

Armchair journeys – sitting down all the time (cruise or rail)

Where you do as little activity as possible, including sight-seeing. Armchair travelers do travel, but they don't like standing up or walking and God forbid anyone should ask them to run, hike, ski, or make a decision.

Dinner party journeys – Hyacinthe Bouquet

Related to ego trips, but you don't actually do half the things you say you do – you just talk about them afterwards. You know the type. They ask you to dinner or you ask them to dinner and they talk about the hotel, the cost of the hotel, where they went what they did, the cost of what they did. Who else has been there, preferably famous, and what they hope to do next year. What it will cost to do next year. They will never ask you where you are going, what you did, or what you want to do.

Box of chocolate journeys

Journeys you only enjoy some of, either because you have to rough it, or because you only organized part of it yourself (some of it is to please the partner or friends you are traveling with). Also journeys you take with someone who you love most of the time, and find really irritating at other times.

SHIRLY VALENTINE Journeys

Little life, big adventure. Life changing, mind altering journeys that change the way we think about ourselves, increasing compassion for ourselves and for others.

Empty bucket journeys – bucket list journeys that are clichéd

Most overrated journeys are those you felt you ought to take before you die. Overrated because you expect the top ten in everything, but travel is subjective. Some people go 'wow' at the Grand Canyon, others would prefer to watch a computer game.

Round the world journeys

As in going round in circles and seeing everything. These are journeys where you end up where you started – as in emotionally, intellectually and physically. It has merely reinforced what you already know and feel. You are passing the time.

Mirror-mirror journeys – looking at yourself as opposed to ego trips: real self discovery

You're lost in life. You don't know what to do or where to go, and you need direction. You want to get some sense of self back. Usually to places such as India where you seek self-awareness, but in truth, can be anywhere you find a connection to the land and culture and discover more about yourself by the way you react to the culture/people/challenges.

ABC journeys (random)

Journeys taken for no reason other than they are cheap, half price, and within your budget and time constraints. Usually highly repetitive and uninspiring. Those who return to the same place every year at the same time or who like beach and villa holidays take ABC journeys.

Pincushion journeys – with someone you hate

Who would go traveling with someone you hate? A lot of us actually, although we rarely discover that until we have traveled with them. Usually happens with acquaintances as you discover you have different views on budget, holiday, childcare, fun, and values. Only go traveling with those you love. Even if that means only going on holiday by yourself.

Jellyfish journeys – traveling with friends

Beautiful and deadly, killing friendships unless you are the same or compliment each other and agree to 'go with the flow'. The expectation of joy when traveling with friends is usually so high, nothing is able to match it. Keep expectations low and all will be well.

Bryson journeys

Because Bill Bryson says so, or any 'expert' says so. You are following someone else's advice about going to a place or destination. On recommendation, so if it's no good you can blame someone else.

Two: Travelling With Your Emotions

•

"Just go with an open mind and when the going gets tough, keep going, because you'll get through it."
Duncan Goose, CEO of One Brand, who last year raised £10 million improving water supplies in Africa.

Anxious, depressed, lonely, heartbroken, grief stricken, tired, lacking in focus, sad, unbalanced, hateful, jealous, envious, greedy, self-obsessed, lazy, vain, impatient, vengeful? Or all of the above?

Stand back from the emotion and look at it as though it doesn't belong to you. As though you have the feeling in your hand and want to study it rather than feel it. Take this 'feeling' with you on your journey and leave it there. Let it go there. And come back with less emotional baggage than you went. And ps, don't pick up anyone elses' either.

ANXIOUS?

Will you catch the flight, will the train be on time, do you have the right travel insurance, will the sun shine. Holidays create stress and anxiety even before you start booking. So choosing the right company that treats you as an individual, not a number, that is able to ease your journey from start to finish and chosing a destination and a culture that makes anxiety a redundant emotion to feel – not just there, but when you return as well.

JOURNEYS THAT WORK

Octopus journeys

Where you have a lot of fingers in lots of pies, but you are grounded and centred. You always return to one base where everything is done for you and you go wild during the day. Its important to have both elements so that when you return home to that unnecessary nuisance called responsibility you don't fall apart.

Hedgehog journeys

Release anxiety by confronting things head on. Building up the training to refocus the mind and have time for nothing other than the challenges ahead. Doesn't let go of the fact you still have the capability to be anxious, but better prepares you for challenges in future.

Serendipity journeys

Journeys you feel that were meant to be. That were fortuitous you took them, when you take them by chance. I interviewed Tara Palmer Tomkinson once and asked her what she did on holidays. "I go to the airport, think of a number between one and fifty than then count down on the departure board. Whatever is the number I go for it. Perhaps not that day, but the next. I just go. Few have that luxury but it takes the stress out of the research bit. And you can adapt the principle.

GO FOR – trekking and adventure holidays, holidays with a guide with a small group or one on one. Can be anywhere. Hot or cold climate irrelevant. Outdoor and wilderness holidays.

AVOID – holidays with the family or friends you want/feel need to impress, all inclusive, cruises because they don't confront the issue – they allow you to ignore it.

DEPRESSED?

Moroseness, despondency, agitation, not wanting to get out of bed, the list of symptoms is endless but initially starts with a prolonged lack of self confidence. Clinical depression is go to the doctor territory. The irony is therapists will tell you that they are told never to tell you if you are depressed. You should be telling yourself that. But if you feel a continued sense of worthlessness, either want to eat everything or nothing, have loss appetite for life as well as food – then you may be depressed.

JOURNEYS THAT WORK

Onion journeys

We allow our emotions to release in layers. We unfold when we feel more relaxed about opening up and journeys allow us to do that through time. When you travel with other people their emotional baggage may rebound onto you. You may also dump your baggage onto them - albeit subconsciously. They are not counsellors (unless of course, they are!). Most people speak from their own experience, nothing more. Travel with interesting people or a guide.

Walkabout journeys

That film *Walkabout*. Remember the sense of fear that they had initially when they were lost and then they had an adventure. Actress Jenny Agutter playing one of the children stranded in the Outback with her brother, at the end of the film her character was seen to be safe in a small apartment and dreamt of her time in the open wilderness. It was a rather depressing ending as it showed the scale of her adventure compared to her small life now. It was there she learnt the most, lived the most. Remember the low times because it is frequently in these times you learn and grow the most. Imagination flows when you are miserable.

Remember the tough journeys you take, it is here you will learn the most.

Jam jar journeys

So called because you look as though you are having a fabulous time, but in truth you are trapped. You are in the sweet 'jam' but you are stuck in it. Hence, luxury holidays do not suit those who are in a state of depression. You are have paid top dollar to be happy which only makes the situation worse. Travel is one of those things that the more you pay, it doesn't necessarily mean you will get more from it.

GO FOR – wilderness, outdoor adventure, white water rafting, holidays that present a physical challenge and release. Ideally warm but not hot climate. Go by self but within a group. Ranching holidays (being around horses is known to alleviate depression and other emotional negativity).

AVOID – family holidays and holidays with friends, cruises, all inclusive as they allow you too much thinking time and you will be prone to deal with their issues rather than your own if traveling with family and friends.

LONELY?

You will be alone in a crowd so don't choose anywhere with loads of people. Cities can be fun and exciting but also leave you feeling 'out of it' if you don't choose a culture that encourages conversation in the cafes, and where people smile at you in the street not because they want to steal your purse or wallet but because they have nothing to prove or hide. This leaves out most of the western cities known to man. But leaves wide open for discovery the wide open spaces where you ironically feel less alone.

JOURNEYS THAT WORK

Cuddle journeys

Wilderness and nature and empty spaces cuddle you more effectively than places where there are a lot of people. Nature cuddles, cities do not.

Book mark journeys

Journeys that have regular stops to allow you to pause for thought and contemplate what you have done, who you have met and where you are going.

Paper weight journeys

Journeys that ground you and your thoughts. Feeling lonely is nothing to do with other people, its all to do with being happy with your own company. These journeys focus on improving sense of self identity and self worth.

GO FOR – adventure trekking – but ones that start at one point and end at another (do not go on one where you are going in a 'circle' – ie end up where you started – this is psychologically not good). Cold or warm climate – not hot. In a group no smaller than four no larger than ten.

AVOID – city breaks as you are always most lonely in a crowd and with someone you don't love. There is no exception to this rule.

HEARTBROKEN?

You can't stop thinking about him? Or her? One of the reasons I wrote this book is because I couldn't stop thinking about the ex and then I took a trip to China and suddenly it put my feelings into perspective. There was something about the culture that weakened the emotion. Go somewhere where the fairy tale notion of romance and love is turned on its head – and so will you be.

JOURNEYS THAT WORK

Paper trail journeys

Journeys where you can't go as a couple because it would restrict you. Adventurous solo journeys where you have to navigate by yourself. You are on a solo journey and no one can take it for you.

Dragon journeys

Culture shock, where emotion is treated differently to the western world of heartbreak, works well. Think China where there are far more important things to sob over, and you get the idea.

Back bend journeys

Journeys that make you vulnerable. Shock but in a different way. Returning to those places you went as a couple but go as a single. NOT AS ANOTHER COUPLE. But as a single. You will see it differently but not in the way you think. By making yourself vulnerable you make yourself stronger. Like when you do back bends in yoga, it releases tension.

GO FOR – high adventure or high culture as in dramatically different culture (eg China). Europe is not sufficiently different and distracting. Hot or cold climate.

AVOID – purpose built 'singles holidays'. Heartbreak should be distracted, not compounded by stating the obvious. European breaks. City breaks.

GRIEF-STRICKEN?

An overwhelming uncontrollable sense of loss that nothing and no one is able to help you with. There are seven recognised stages of grief - denial, guilt, anger, depression, upward turn, working through and acceptance. However it is not a straight forward journey from denial to hope and acceptance. You may see-saw backwards and forwards between guilt and anger, anger and denial and guilt and depression. A change of direction and focus, a constant distraction that makes you think in a different way. It is thinking in a different way that

will make you feel a different way. Journeys do that –
some journeys do that.

JOURNEYS THAT WORK

Simon Cowell journeys

Not that this personality gives you grief (well he does
to some), but he points out the un-PC truth, even if
it's brutal about a situation or person. They say you
learn most from those who hurt you the most, which I
think should be on Simon Cowell's grave stone, but
there is an element of truth in this. Wood for the trees,
however you want to put it, people are blinded by
grief. Journeys that allow you to see the bigger
picture without the platitudes of 'light end of tunnel',
resonate with those who sense nothing other than the
sorrow they feel.

Stroke journeys

When intellectualizing the sorrow doesn't work,
journeys that appeal to the emotions work.

ET journeys

Journeys which take you out of yourself and
comfort zone.

**GO FOR – adventure and wilderness holidays –
the more wild and dramatic the better. The
landscape will literally 'absorb' the emotion. You
will become like blotting paper emotionally, taking**

in what nature has to offer. (eg Yukon, Australian outback, genuine rather than cultivated wilderness – ie National Parks no good other than in States and Canada where 'park' is wilderness). Climate irrelevant. Small groups. Recommended guide.

AVOID holidays which focus on WWI and WWII history or any war for that matter. Anything that smacks of 'loss'. No war memorials!

ANGRY?

Anger internalized turns to depression. Constant anger may make you happy, but for those around you it's a pain. You are a pain to work with, live with and it's a weakness. All bullies eventually get found out in the playground at school, in the gym, in the home and the office. You may not want to go on this journey but those around you will want you to.

JOURNEYS THAT WORK

Pressure cooker journeys

Journeys that touch upon the symptoms of the anger. Anger is derived from fear. Fear is the opposite of love. Men get angry when they are afraid. Women cry when they are angry. So men look angry and women look afraid when in fact, it is the other way round. Journeys which push your button straight away and go to the heart of the matter. These journeys need a guide or role model that does that. And allows the anger to release into an environment able to absorb it like blotting paper.

Up/down journeys

Anger is a positive emotion. Internalised it becomes depression but it is a powerful energy able to move mountains or start wars. Or end them. Directed in the right way it can enable you to achieve more than you anticipated. Climbing or descending channels the mind, and focuses the activity. The anger has an outlet. Any journeys that take you high and lead you down again are essentially grounding and focus you on wondering what all your fuss was about.

Sharp nail journeys

Sharp nail as when you step on one with bare feet and it's a short sharp shock to the system. It makes you realize you should have been wearing shoes and looking where you were going. Journeys that make you do this work with anger management issues because they make you realize very quickly that there is something bigger out there than your anger and teach you to be more aware of what is around you and the impact you are having on others.

GO FOR – Mountain climbing, white water rafting, Indiana Jones type adventure. No frills. OK, only on the last day as a reward if you must. Ranching holidays rather than riding holidays. Ideally cool to cold climate.

AVOID – luxury holidays, all inclusive, cruises too much thinking time and feeling of enclosure – either because of geography (stuck on ship), or need to make the most of the 'value for money' element of the break – ie all inclusive – must eat as much as possible; or luxury – must take full advantage of what is on offer within the 'deal'.

TIRED?

Constantly tired, lack luster, wanting to kick yourself up the backside you are so slow of thought, of word, of action. No amount of caffeine-infused drink will keep you going or you don't want to always use this way of keeping yourself on the ball. Some destinations leave you needing a holiday when you return – even those which call themselves 'retreats'. The following journeys will invigorate and energize - and they don't even say that on the brochure.

WHAT JOURNEYS WORK

Caffeine journeys

Journeys that make you feel as though you've been injected with caffeine – put you on a high.

Reject journeys

Journeys that make you understand that the path you have been on is making you tired and that you need to reboot and refocus in a new direction.

Sherbet dib-dab journeys

Everyone has a different way of eating sherbet dib dab. Using the licorice stick, putting it all in your mouth at once, or using your finger to get out the sherbet. Journeys that make you realize there is more than one way to do something and ignite your imagination.

GO FOR – wilderness journeys, small groups, or ideally one on one. travel with your teenager if you have one. Any type of climate.

AVOID Cruises, self catering, luxury, camping, family holidays. family holidays add to the fatigue. Ditto self catering. Luxury holidays and cruising don't allow you to work through it, they merely allow the 'tiredness' to be more sustainable. (ie they don't deal with the cause just the symptom and its only temporary).

LACKING FOCUS?

So you went upstairs for something and by the time you got up there, you forgot what you went there for. What was it? Preoccupied, mind elsewhere, too much on your mind, and achieving nothing. Taking a holiday is the last thing you can afford to do as you have so much to do and don't know where to start. But taking the right journey focuses the mind.

WHAT JOURNEYS WORK

Stretch 'n Shape journeys

Nothing to do with a fitness workout, but to do with hyper extending our bodies, and minds, and over stretching ourselves for the sake of 'keeping high' and not focused. Lack of focus comes from too much going on, and not knowing where to start, lack of prioritizing, and being distracted. Giving too much when you don't have enough time for yourself. These journeys allow you to focus on you (as opposed to anger management type journeys which focus you on others).

Open book journeys

Journeys that make you look at yourself as though you are the protagonist in a soap opera and you are observing yourself. Are you happy being that character? Would you like to be someone else or indeed in the soap opera at all. Journeys that take you out of yourself and allow you to look at yourself.

Looking glass journeys

More house of mirrors, these journeys show what you can achieve when focused and why you lack focus. On these journeys they make you focus on one thing at a time – otherwise you let the team down.

GO FOR – three day short break cultural trips to high impact culture cities (Vienna, Venice, St

Petersburg, New York, Barcelona, Prague for example). Organise one on one guide for three days. Learning to sail holidays. Holidays with your teenager. Cool to warm climate – not extremes.

AVOID – all inclusive, luxury holidays, cruises as there are few distractions to challenge the issue. Family holidays.

SAD?

Three simple letters yet its one emotion women tend to 'stick' at and men never reach (they usually stick on 'anger') when they are recovering from any disappointment. Seasonal affective disorder can happen even when the sun is shining.

WHAT JOURNEYS WORK

Telescope journeys

Journeys that make the things that seem out of reach much closer.

Angel journeys

Journeys that are high up for one reason or another – think mountains, sky diving, paragliding, anything to do with 'flying' free.

Apple pie journeys

Journeys that focus on the sensual elements of life – smells, tastes, sounds and touch.

GO FOR – paragliding, sky diving, anything to do with flying (in a plane doesn't count). Trips with one on one guides. Outdoor walking, cycling, riding. Ranching holidays in Canada and USA– genuine ranches rather than the 'cosmetic'. Climate irrelevant – but ideally 'bright' (ie bright winter light or Spring light).

AVOID – city breaks, self catering holidays, single holidays as cities create a sense of loneliness, self catering holidays allow too much thinking time, ditto singles holidays.

UNBALANCED

Do you feel totally unaligned? Work-life balance screwed? Can't see the children enough, the partner enough, or achieve enough at work? Time management all over the place? Feeling up one moment and down the next?

WHAT JOURNEYS WORK

Typewriter journeys

So called because you have so much to say and do, you don't know where to start. Slowing down and carefully spelling out what you need is the answer. Journeys which force you to slow down are ideal.

Warrior journeys

Journeys where aggression is essential to move on. You are fighting in someway and it is essential to use that aggression to stay focused.

White water journeys

Or roller coaster – ups and downs all the time and the pace slows and quickens. It allows the person to appreciate stillness, calm and routine.

GO FOR – white water, mountaineering, trekking, cultures known for their passion for life – think South America. Cold or hot climate.

AVOID – camping holidays (they don't test you enough), self catering for families, family holidays, any sort of self catering holiday. Families create distraction and add to the imbalance. Camping holidays in particular do this especially if you are the chief carer (the woman/the mother).

HATEFUL?

The world is full of too much hate. Hate is created by fear. Fear is the opposite of love. Think about that one. Those who are hateful are afraid. It must be utterly exhausting to be hateful all the time. And there are some very good haters about. They attack all the time. The late President Nixon, a man not well known for his interpersonal skills, but who managed to thaw the 'hateful' relationship (some would say) between China and the States, famously said, 'Always give your best, never get discouraged, never be petty; always remember, others may hate you, but those who hate you don't win unless you hate them, and then you destroy yourself.' That is always, without exception, true.

WHAT JOURNEYS WORK

Hedgehog journeys

Think of a hedgehog. All prickles and picks up stuff along the way because of its spikes, but actually hedgehogs do a lot of good. And they're soft at heart. Hedgehog journeys do that as well. They appear challenging but they are good for you and they know when enough is enough. Hedgehog journeys teach compassion for self by showing us how our actions may hurt others.

Clown journeys

Humour breaks through hate. The clown is more powerful than the adventurer but the two combined pack a powerful punch. So any journey that has whimsy to it, has humorous and unexpected twists and turns and a positive slant will always cut through hateful thought.

Snow White journeys

Being the baddy. The wicked witch. Hateful people realize they are hateful and visualize themselves as the baddy, thereby sustaining the emotion as well as the image. But all that hate is exhausting. In their own way, they want to be rescued from themselves. Journeys that show them how their energy can be better spent is more useful and constructive.

GO FOR – holidays that require lots of physical energy – high adventure, white water, mountaineering, kayaking, ranching, holidays with animals – not looking at them – working with them and helping them. Cold to cool climates.

AVOID – Luxury holidays, self-catering, hotel holidays, family holidays, self catering. Romantic breaks. Staying away from other people, wilderness holidays absorb the hate – other people will reflect it.

JEALOUS

Jealousy is when you want to be someone else or have something that someone else has and you don't want that person to have it. Think car, job, boyfriend, girlfriend, looks, slim waist, happy marriage.

It's one of the most destructive emotions. Any 'self help' book will tell you that it's the only emotion that doesn't have a 'purpose' – an upside to move you forward and on, it holds you back, keeps you from progressing or taking any form of emotional journey.

WHAT JOURNEYS WORK

Jab-Jab Punch journeys

Jealousy is the one emotion that has no upside to feeling it. Most emotions are transitional and have an upside, but jealousy has none. Any journey that knocks the wind out of the emotion will move you on from the emotion. When feelings of jealousy are made to seem irrelevant or unnecessary, they dissipate. Journeys that involve gaining of self-esteem, self worth and perspective.

Matchbox journeys

Jealousy essentially means you want to be someone you are not or have something you do not. If you were happy with yourself you wouldn't feel the need for someone else's quality – you would be happy with your own. So why aren't you happy with yourself? What is wrong with you? If you are jealous, you are unhappy with yourself. These journeys look at the little things about yourself that you miss. The details. It brings out the things you would rather hide, keep in a box hidden away until the box is so full, they explode. You need a safe place for them to explode.

Alien vs Predator journeys

Journeys which confront the jealousy. Jealous of wealth, of health, of happiness, you go on the journeys where they are full of each and see for yourself that the grass isn't greener – because it never is.

GO FOR – wilderness holidays, walking holidays anywhere, small groups or one on one with a guide who is passionate about what they know as well as knowledgeable. Places where the obvious wealth is obscene – nothing like force-feeding someone with a sweet tooth, chocolate for days on end. Cool climates.

AVOID – back packing holidays. They will make you think of what you could have had. You will have too much 'thinking time'.

ENVIOUS?

Envy is when you want something that someone else has got. It differs from jealousy in that you are happy for the other person to have what you covet, you just want it as well. Jealousy you don't want the person to have what they've got – you want to be better than them. With envy, you are happy to be the same as them. It may not be right for you but you want it. It's not that you don't want them to have it as well – you are fine with that. You just want it (that's how envy differs from jealousy). Celebrity culture has nurtured this.

I tell my son everything he sees advertised in between the programmes is stuff he will never need or should want. If it was, they wouldn't need to advertise it. And that he should never be envious of other people because what you see is only the tip of the iceberg – good and bad. No life is perfect. Nothing tells you that more than taking a journey. The appropriate journeys teach you perspective, purpose and worth of self and what is around you.

WHAT JOURNEYS WORK

Playground journeys

Journeys that make you realize how childish and spiteful your envy is.

Spell check journeys

Journeys that spell out the implications and consequences of envy – as in losing friends, gaining enemies, not able to focus on the positive.

Coconut journeys

Journeys that show there is nothing to envy about anyone and what is perceived to be desirable rarely is – i.e. the dream is a hollow one, lacking in substance.

GO FOR – back packing, simple trekking (basic no luxury), train journeys, cycling, climbing, hiking but with a mission at the end of it – ie you are doing it for charity that will help someone somewhere in the world. Ie your journey is for a greater good, not just yours. Cool climates.

AVOID Cruising, luxury, camping, family, self-catering. Too much time to think and too much that may be related to directly what you are envious about.

GREEDY/SELF-OBSESSED?

For food and for money. For other peoples time (impatient and self obsessed). Hedonistic. It's all about you, has always been about you. Will always be about you. Then if you don't recognize it, then someone else will.

JOURNEYS THAT WORK

Sand dune journeys

Journeys where there seems to be nothing you want to eat but there could be if you go that extra mile. It is all about the destination, achieving the goal but the journey becomes more interesting along the route. The motivation is to get over the next hurdle, but in the end you enjoy the hurdles more than the anticipation of what is over the other side.

Motorway journeys

Similar to sand dune journeys but easier to navigate. So easy you are able to go great distances but you need to do it fast. You have no time to think of anything else as the journey is all about speed.

Mrs Norris journeys

Mrs Norris is a character in a novel by Jane Austen (Mansfield Park), a snob who appears harmless, but is in fact spiteful. She humiliates the other characters. Journeys that starve people who are greedy of what they most want, makes them want it more. It effectively becomes a humiliation. Those journeys that show them how by changing their ways will help them is more effective.

GO FOR – any holiday where there is a need for speed and preferably you are doing it for charity and not just yourself. Rally car holidays, open top journeys through USA, RV journey in Canada, dune buggy journeys in desert, outback journeys in Australia, any form of holiday where a 'race' is involved in some way. Cool to warm climates.

AVOID – all-inclusive and cruises. Anything that resembles any form of rambling and slow paced holiday. Health farm holidays, or anything akin to it. All inclusive and cruises there's as much food as you can eat all the time even if you don't want it. And health farm holidays increase the craving for food rather than decrease it. Slow paced holidays will allow more time to eat.

LAZY?

You would rather get someone else to breathe for you if you could afford it. It's not a case of fatigue, or lack of ability, more a case that you ,for one reason or another, can offload all your work load – and life if needs be – onto other people. You have no sense of independence and, what's more, don't want to.

WHAT JOURNEYS WORK

Find the bear journeys

Where you have to take another step to find what you are looking for – it is never waiting for you. And what you are looking for is always on the move and arrives when you least expect it. Like a bear it could also attack you. So you need to be alert.

Journeys where you are on a mission.

Goldfish journeys

Are you in the bowl or are you looking into the bowl? Journeys that change perspective.

Hot carrot journeys

Journeys that kick start even the laziest person into action motivating by use of carrot and stick.

GO FOR – third world country adventure, wilderness adventure, mountaineering, volunteering. Cold to cool climates.

AVOID – luxury holidays and all inclusive. Everyone does everything for you on these types of holiday. They cater for and nurture sloth and laziness.

VAIN?

Mirror, mirror on the wall, you are the smoothest, most selfish of them all. You need to look good all the time, preen and perfect. It's all about looks. But they fade. Even with botox they fade. So you gain perspective again.

JOURNEYS THAT WORK

Malificent journeys

Journeys that show you as you truly are, not what you think you are or what you would like to be.

Monte Carlo journeys

Journeys where you fit in, and are even outdone. As in, those around you are even more vain than you are.

Frog journeys

So called because the frog is better than the prince. As in what looks good isn't always right for you.

GO FOR – race journeys (i.e. some form of challenge to complete), white water, ranching (but as a helper/wrangler), wilderness journeys but on a mission and where you need to rough it and be part of a team. Hot or cold climate.

AVOID – Monte Carlo, Dubai, Las Vegas, Milan, anywhere where people are self-obsessed and not self aware.

IMPATIENT?

You want to get there now, you can't wait, you must be first, it's a race against time, no against yourself. And everyone is going in s-l-o-w m-o-t-i-o-n. and the driver in front, if they drove any slower, would go backwards. Why can't everyone be more efficient? What is wrong with this place? Try another one.

WHAT JOURNEYS WORK

Car crash journeys

Where you have to slow down and be patient because if you don't you put yourself and others at risk.

Red vase journeys

Waiting for something to come along you've ordered. Like an red vase on ebay. Checking to make sure its there and doing something while you are waiting. Journeys that make you use your time more effectively so you don't realize you are 'waiting' at all. Even holiday you have to save up for years.

Teapot journeys

Too hot to pour at the moment, so you've got to wait. Journeys that require planning and training before you go on them.

GO FOR – wilderness adventure, learn to sail holidays, white water rafting, mountaineering, third world country expeditions. Hot or cold climates.

AVOID – Luxury holidays, cruising. Luxury holidays everything is pampered for, ditto cruising, there is no element of DIY.

VENGEFUL?

Completely overwhelms all actions and thoughts. This can motivate you into action and limit you. It is useless telling someone who is vengeful not to bother – and that karma will work. They will tell you, they know, but by the time it does, they won't care. In the meantime – just take the right trips.

JOURNEYS THAT WORK

Bunny boiler journeys

Journeys that make you laugh about your feelings. Think murder mystery weekends.

Hero journeys

Journeys that make a hero or heroine out of you – because you achieve something. Why be vengeful when there is so much else to feel grateful and happy about?

Captain, my captain journeys

Not journeys with friends but journeys where you make friends. Think role model journeys, Indiana Jones and Croc Dundee, Dead Poets Society. No time for revenge.

GO FOR – wilderness adventures where there is a 'captain, my captain' of a guide (ie Croc Dundee and Indiana Jones – substance as well as style – must have both). Ranching holidays as a wrangler. Cold to cool climates.

AVOID – holidays with families or friends, or self catering, cruising or luxury which allow too much thinking time. And families and friends may encourage vengeful thoughts rather than alleviate them – albeit unintentionally.

THREE: PACKING THE EMOTIONAL BAGGAGE

A journey is a person in itself, no two are alike, and all plans, safeguards, policies and coercion are fruitless. We find after years of struggles that we do not take trips; a trip takes us.
John Steinbeck

HOW TO PACK THE EMOTIONAL BAGGAGE WHEN TRAVELLING

I have written over the years so many top-ten tips on how to travel, where to travel, how to travel with a baby, toddler, teenager, parent, grand parent, long haul, short haul, pack, unpack, camping, cruising, hot climate, cold climate, all very prescriptive but none dealing with the nitty gritty of emotions and thoughts. You may be able to afford to go to the most luxurious place with a loved one, but if you are not in the right place mentally, you will not be in the right place physically.

You may visit the most romantic destination as defined by Conde Nast Traveller, but if you have fallen out of love with the person who is taking you there, you are better off staying at home. The free tan is not worth it.

These are the REALLY important factors to take into account when travelling. Forget how to pack your suitcase, focus on your own emotional baggage first.

PPP people, pace, pennies

People:

Who are you traveling with? Do you really get on with them? What is their budget? Do you like their children, if they are going with you? How well do you know them? Why are you going with them – money to share cost or friendship? Are they traveling with you for the same reason? Do you believe them? What are they like under stress? How long you going for? Can you hold your emotional breath that long?

Pace:

How long are you giving yourself? Have you done this journey before? Have you given yourself rest stops? Are you competing with time, with yourself, or no one? Is it the right time for you to go on a trip like this? Trust your instinct on this one.

Pennies:

Are you working within budget? How do you know? Have you considered all the what ifs? If you are focusing on the money to the exclusion of everything else, you will always be focusing on the money and not the experience. Think about that. It will spoil your trip. You are not focusing on the experience you are focusing on the cost of the experience and not the value of it. Your mindset will be different, distorted. You are not focusing on its worth but on its cost. It may cost £100 or £10,000, but both trips can be over-priced and under-valued if you focus on the £££.

FAB: family, acquaintances, buddies

Do you know these people because you have to or because you choose to? Family – do you really want to travel with your family? Why are you doing it? Why are they doing it? How well do you know them? Are you doing it because you want to get to know them better? Why do you need a journey to do that? Acquaintances are so called because you tolerate them for a short amount of time and they are not good people in times of crisis, so why go on holiday with them? They will let you down. Friends are good to travel with – and you will find out exactly how good or bad they are when doing so.

OYS – older, younger, same

Age is a number. Level of fitness, values, and budget are more important. But you can learn so much from those much older and much younger than you. When you travel with someone your age, you are competing with yourself.

TEC – target task; explore, expand; contract, conclude

What do you want to achieve by the journey? What do you want to discover – about the place, about yourself? Where to do you want to be at the end of it, emotionally? What do you want to achieve? Do you want to achieve anything? If not, why are you doing it? Where do you emotionally, physically, intellectually and spiritually want to end up?

AGO – aims, goals, objectives

Do you have any, even if it's just to have a 'good time'? What is a 'good time' in your opinion? Looking at it, do you really think it's enough?

HV (high value), LV (low value)

What is important about the journey – the deal breakers and makers? What is high value to you (cost, person, timing) and what is low value (i.e. points to consider but not deal breakers (type of hotel, where you eat, what you do each day).

Exlectics – be positive

Everyone has a **POV** (point of view). It's not a case of you are right and they are wrong when deciding on a journey – if you are traveling with someone else. Take the best bits – the gold dust – from both of your ideas and amalgamate. Not compromise – malgamate. Professor Edward de Bono mentions the Japanese way of making decisions called 'Exlectics', which focuses on the good in all opinions and works to a common good. Same with journeys. Don't think of it as compromise if you want to go to the States and your loved one wants to go to France. What is it about both destinations that fulfills each of your needs ? Romance? Adventure? Comfort? Find the common denominators – the positives. Then identify the USPs (unique selling points) the differences, or minus points of each (you may not think of them as minus points just interesting points) and then see if there is another destination that fulfills all.

> **EBS** – examine both sides.
> **PMI** – positive, minus, interesting.
> **CAF** – consider all factors

ME, MYSELF, I

If you were looking on at yourself, would you like to travel with you? Who do you feel wouldn't want to travel with you and why? Do they have a point about not wanting to travel with you? Would it be best to travel by yourself?

FOUR: TRAVEL MYTHS

The best place I've been to in the world is always the next place I'm going to.
Michael Palin

TRAVEL MYTHS

Many myths surround travel, mainly because there is an element of fantasy about it and we, the punter, are complicit in that fantasy. We want and expect the people we meet to be friendly, the weather to be wonderful, the sea to be warm. We have such high expectations of holidays that we don't want to take risks, especially if we have only two weeks to take our main annual break. The first week is usually spent becoming relaxed – the second week is when the holiday actually begins. So traveling to the same destination year on year is less to do with lack of imagination or even lack of budget than with being risk averse. How many of us will travel to Antarctica? How many will trek through the Galapagos, or go bear hunting in the Yukon? What is important is to debunk the myths, to see travel for what it really is, and what the experience really offers – an opportunity to get rid of emotional baggage.

MYTH NUMBER ONE: THE WORLD HAS GOT SMALLER

The world has not got smaller, just our ability to see it. Travel changes what you think and feel, rather than what you see and do.

MYTH NUMBER TWO: MEN CONQUER, WOMEN FOLLOW

Wrong. Women make exemplary travellers. Their innate ability to think laterally, when focused on themselves and their own needs as opposed to the needs of their mother, lover, boyfriend, husband, someone else's husband, children, grandparent, boss, Victoria Beckham, in fact anyone other than themselves, they are able to conquer anything.

MYTH NUMBER THREE: PEOPLE WHO TRAVEL MORE ARE MORE WORLDLY

Nope. It's not that you've taken the test, it's what you've learnt from it. As soon as you are able to afford luxury, you put yourself inside the goldfish bowl. In fact not even a goldfish bowl because you can't see outside properly. Take this example. A Russian family wanted to see gorillas. They booked a lodge and private helicopter and guides. When the gorillas were spotted, the helicopter came to collect them, dropped them into the jungle and left them there to see the gorillas. When they had become bored, they were airlifted out and taken back to their lodge. Like a zoo without the bars, and just as much fun. Just as money can't buy you taste (ask any interior designer who has been commissioned by a wealthy client), it can't buy the ability to appreciate what is around you. In many ways, it's that quality of being totally self-absorbed that helps many to accumulate their millions. So to expect them to suddenly be aware and compassionate to what is around them when they've had a lifetime of 'me, me, me' is a big ask. Travel widens perspectives and horizons only if you are open to it and you leave your ego at home.

MYTH NUMBER FOUR: TRAVEL WRITERS AND EXPERTS KNOW BETTER THAN YOU

I may be shooting myself in the foot here, but this is not true. Travel writing is subjective, it is never objective. Travel writers have frequently seen too much of the world and take it for granted – nothing is wonderful any more – or they may have an agenda to follow belonging to their editor/publisher/paper. I took up writing novels because I wanted to write the truth. The irony was, I had to call it 'fiction'.

Everyone has a different perspective on a place or journey and even if the majority say one thing, it doesn't mean the majority is correct. The travel writer may be able to express their subjective view in a highly articulate, amusing way, but it is still just their opinion. Also, the media is incredibly fickle. Only five years ago you would have never considered holidaying in Oman, now it's in the top ten of UK holiday destinations. Libya, a country that is now associated with suicide bombers and crumpled buildings, has a history and landscape that surpasses ours a hundredfold (although that's just my opinion). In short, don't believe everything you read. Go visit yourself.

MYTH NUMBER FIVE: THE BEST WAY TO TRAVEL IS BY YOURSELF

This is a bit like the saying 'chocolate is better than sex'. It depends on the chocolate. It depends on the sex. With reference to travelling alone or with someone, the same rule follows. Choose your companion wisely. Your husband or lover isn't always the best. Sisters tend to travel well, in fact some sibling relationships that never work at home or while 'static' work when travelling. It is good to bounce ideas off someone else, but you need to be able to speak up and go your own way if and when you want to. Control-freakish tendencies come out when travelling, so be able to stand up for yourself, and agree to go separate ways. (Unless, of course, you are at the South Pole and your life depends on it).

MYTH NUMBER SIX: YOU HAVE TO SEE ALL THE WONDERS OF THE WORLD BEFORE YOU DIE

No you don't. They are stunning, beautiful, and phenomenal in their own way, but visiting them for the sake of tick-boxing them off in your 'life journey' will not make you a better person. It will make you a person who can say they've been there.

You need a reason.

MYTH NUMBER SEVEN: TRAVEL IS THE ONLY THING YOU BUY THAT MAKES YOU RICHER

No. It's how you perceive it and experience it. There are many platitudes about travel making you see more of life, appreciate it more, and even the famous quote by St Augustine "The world is a book. If you do not travel, you read but a page", isn't true. It depends on the page you read. And those who have travelled the world may have only skimmed the book for stuff they felt they needed or recognised, so using the analogy, I would say, no, travel doesn't make you richer, but it can do.

MYTH NUMBER EIGHT: YOU WILL FEEL ROMANTIC IF YOU GO SOMEWHERE ROMANTIC

No, you will feel romantic if you are romantic and you are with someone you love. You will see the romance in place that others find dull. It is nothing to do with where you are, it is to do with who you are and who you are at the time you visit the place. You are many different people during your lifetime – during your development. You are not the same person at twenty, thirty or forty. There are some of you who will see the romance in a wet windy day on a beach in Norfolk and others who will think 'this is cold and miserable'. There are others who will feel loved-up walking along a beach in the Seychelles, others who will think it's hyped-up manufactured romance at a ridiculous price. This is not to do with the place, it's to do with you and your perception of the place. Even cities such as Paris, Rome and Florence are lacklustre if you are in the wrong place emotionally.

MYTH NUMBER NINE: A CHANGE IS AS GOOD AS A REST

What does that mean? A rest is only good when you have a change? What sort of change? A change in how you feel, where you are, where you want to be, an opinion, an attitude, a place, a job, a partner? A change of any sort? And what sort of a rest? A rest from the rat race? From repetition? From the norm? From your friends and family, your job, your life? The platitude means nothing. A change is not as good as a rest. A rest is not as good as a change. It's nonsense. It's not even a myth.

MYTH NUMBER TEN: YOU'VE GOT TO ROUGH IT TO SEE A PLACE PROPERLY

No, you've got to be in the right place to see a place properly. And what is seeing a place properly? It is identifying how that place, that moment in time can help you. Money doesn't mean the experience will be better, but it doesn't mean it will be less rewarding either, for all those trekking snobs out there.

Those were the myths. Now for the wisdom. I prefer wisdom to tips. It's something you've known all along, a voice telling you inside it's right, you just need a nudging.

FIVE: TRAVEL WISDOMS

The things you most regret in life are the things you didn't do, not the things you did. Be bold. Have the baby, go to the Galapagos, get your boobs enhanced, sleep with your boss, move in with the postman – whatever. Don't spend an old age moaning "If only I had". The less you play safe, the richer your life – and for all you know, the postman will win the lottery anyway."
Fay Weldon

TRAVEL WISDOMS

This chapter focuses on specific journeys I have taken over the years that have worked for me, and how they have helped. The 'SUGGESTED JOURNEYS' are taken from my travel diaries while on location which worked for me or my colleagues over the years. They deal with everything from finding focus, direction and passion to dealing with loneliness and sense of loss. These are merely suggestions, but they show how and why a journey has the power to have an emotional impact as opposed to just seeing and doing interesting things along the way.

TRAVEL WISDOM NUMBER ONE: TRAVEL HEALS THE SOUL

Literal journeys focus the mind on the physical, but in a subliminal way they move someone on emotionally and mentally. Rivers are in constant motion larger than streams which flow fast but narrow, and different from lakes which look still and stagnant, and oceans which are turbulent or quiet, 'deep as the ocean'. Even a beach grows and shrinks with the tides, determined by the movement of the moon, which dictates emotion. In the Far East, 'water' symbolises emotion, and feelings, and a river flowing means that emotions are flowing. Go with the flow, and move with the flow of a river. Cities which face their rivers – Florence, Quebec, even London – have energies different to those cities which lack that free flow of water. These places are good for the soul.

Suggested Journey: UK to Antarctica

London Heathrow, to Buenos Aires, to Ushuaia and beyond…

This is the ultimate in experiential travel. Following in the footsteps of explorers, it's a privilege to be here. It's a place that should leave you cold. Think about it. Loads of ice, blistering cold wind, mammals that may or may not appear (nothing can be fast-tracked), ruddy-faced hardened Russian sailors who will tell you the weather can turn at a blink, birds that swoop by the boats that look small but are in fact of prehistoric size, and terrain that has defeated many men, (but not many women). Nothing may turn up just because you have. The weather may be foul and often is, because it's the South Pole and anything can happen. You can't manage expectations because nature doesn't play to deadlines. The penguins won't appear and waddle on command, nor will whales sound, nor seals peep their grey shiny heads above water and stare at you with those big brown watery eyes of theirs just because you have your camera lens at the ready. To describe Antarctica is difficult. Poets do not do it justice (I've read much of it). Neither do superlatives. But I will try.

We disembarked from the Vavilov, a ship usually used for scientific research for which the past eight days had hosted 92 passengers, ages seven to seventy with 15 nationalities, on a voyage across the Drake Passage to the Antarctic. Or as many of the passengers referred to it, 'the seventh continent' which they had 'done'.

The first day we had 50-knot winds and most of the passengers stayed in their cabins dosed-up on tablets provided by the young doctor (handsome Dr Matt). The birders, an intriguing breed themselves, flocked together getting excited about albatross and terns and other winged creatures which hovered around the boat, ushering us on our way. The Russian captain detoured to miss the worst of the storm but it was all part of the adventure (none of us thought this while we were throwing up, only afterwards, as one would).

Attenborough's *Frozen Planet* sort of prepares you for the first sight of Antarctica. Icebergs like huge Henry Moore sculptures in the ultimate wilderness gallery wait for our zodiacs (black boats where twelve of us sat each day on the edge trying to take photos, watch out for seals, whales, penguins, anything really and take photos without falling off or losing our hats).

If you fall in you will be yanked out by the butt and shoulders and dragged into the centre and then got back on the boat straight away for a hot toddy and hot shower. You will be cold, you will feel ill. So don't fall in. No one fell in.

There was no internet on board the ship for eight days. My son Tom went into serious cold turkey but at least he had computer games that didn't require internet, and the distraction of incredible icebergs, seals, whales and penguins.

Ah, the penguins. We saw about 24,000 of them while we were there. There were a few biologists and eco-scientists qualified up to their woolly hats with PhDs and Masters' who were there to observe. We were there during the hatching season, so saw chicks and various types, Adelie and Chinstraps to name two, none of whom tap-danced. But the way they waddle, they look as though they do.

Two excursions per day, each very different. The most powerful was on Christmas morning when we landed at a former whaling station on Deception

Island. The weather while we had been there had been good – calm seas, easy crossings to land on the zodiacs – but on the morning of the 25th we had wind and heavy snow, almost a white-out. The conditions were fitting as we had learnt about the attempts of Scott and Shackleton and the appalling conditions they dealt with during their expeditions. This was nothing compared to what they had to experience. But as each zodiac landed, on a volcanic beach now thick with snow, – only three penguins there to greet us, the vast empty buildings of the former whaling station the only hint of colour in the monochrome landscape – it was the first time we'd got a taste of what the explorers experienced. We were there for a few hours. Twenty or so decided to skinny-dip (wonderful mad people) but I didn't. Should have done and if you go, do it, because it's mad and then so is bungee jumping.

It's like going to a performance at the opera. The landscape is melodramatic. The space will either draw you in or it won't. It may be your 7th continent to tick-box. The ultimate white Christmas, something to say you've done. Penguins seen. Icebergs climbed. Whale watched. Water jumped into. Tick.

Or you will 'get it'. You will take in everything, sound, sight, smell, touch and you will suffer emotion overload. And you will sob. Not cry, you will sob. Try not to sob when you are out on deck as your tears will freeze. The iceberg backdrop, the whale, the large fat lady who sings, and the penguins: the perpetual chorus line of Charlie Chaplins, waddling and falling over and looking round to see if anyone is looking and then sliding on their bellies, swimming on their backs in the sea, the different species ignoring each other like suburban neighbours comparing wisteria but allowing each other into their space as long as they don't pinch their stones from the nest (they all do it). But I'm projecting personality onto them. They are penguins, fishy-smelling noisy birds that call out and protect their stone nests with determined anality, continually looking at the egg to see if it's still there every few minutes or so just like a mother does her firstborn in the cot. New mothers, you know what I mean.

That relentless wind and cold adds to the drama. Antarctica packs a powerful punch to the stomach, winding you with emotion. Imagine everything that stirs emotion in you all at once, that turns you from the antipathy of anal, relentless, small-minded normality, safety, and fear. Think of something that stirs you with passion, if you know what passion is. Too many places around the world have been described as otherworldly, awesome, phenomenal, stunning, incredible, brilliant, inspiring so to call Antarctica any of these things makes it equivalent, same as, equal to, as good as these places. Comparable to these places. And as interesting as these places probably are in their own way, they are not in this way.

Before I visited, I thought the mountains of ski resorts would have the same or similar energy, or the wonders of the world, and yes, they do lift you – in their own way. Any mountain energy and air lifts you, but it's different here. Think of it, ladies, as a man who tells you he loves you in 'his own way'. That, ladies, as you know, is not love. Now think how you feel when it's the real thing. This is the real thing.

Plus points

It is an extraordinary experience you will only want to do once, and need to do once. It is the closest thing you will get to being on the moon...at the moment.

Minus points

Dull for young children. Expensive.

Interesting points

More mystical than even the documentary series by David Attenborough Frozen Planet.

HV – are you going to go?

A strain on your budget, but with One Oceans it is practical especially if you book flights early.

LV – what may impact on your decision

There will always be reasons not to go – focus on the exclectics and the reasons to go

Alternatives

There is none. This is what makes it so special.

Possibilities

Shortest is an eight-day trip. You can have longer encompassing the Falklands, but that is fourteen to sixteen days and a long time 'at sea'.

Choices

You can go via New Zealand, but it takes considerably longer to reach the Pole than from Patagonia.

TRAVEL WISDOM NUMBER TWO: TRAVEL MAKES YOU MORE INTELLIGENT

I know a lot of well-travelled thick people.

City life excites and focuses some, confuses and irritates others. Country life seems an idyll, but the country life bores and frustrates many who move from an urban community into a rural one where conversation feels narrow and dull, and the quiet is deafening.

"The mind likes to be disciplined like the body," says clinical psychologist, Karen Dempsey, "so challenge it in the same way."

This does not mean different museums every day, or different landscapes.

Suggested Journeys: UK to Venice

Last time I visited was thirty-five years ago. Hot, smelly and following a lady with an umbrella who kept running away from our group, I wasn't impressed by this place that allowed me to walk on water, (well, almost) and wondered why masks and glass were being sold everywhere.

Thirty-five years on, it's very different. I go in January rather than July, when the crowds are limited to the occasional stampede (and they do stampede) of Chinese tourists following a flag – their own, not the red and gold of the extinct Venetian Republic. You don't queue for anything, and you can get into even those tiny restaurants with five tables and waiters who look as if they've lived through several interesting lifetimes

I will get up at 8.30 tomorrow morning when the tide is supposed to be very high, thereby potentially water-logging the bottom floor of my hotel so that the lift has to stop at the first floor and everyone has room service for breakfast. I would have LOVED this as a child. This acqua alta (high water) is happening more frequently when St Marco Square becomes flooded and you wear wellies (always trendy, this is Venice after all).

Everyone is a merchant in Venice but, aware of their own fragility – it is sinking after all – they keep things light. The masks are to hide behind, not just for partying and carnival, because Venice is a village where everyone walks and there is no escape, so everyone knows everyones' business. There was (and is) the guide told me, more than one Casanova. Isn't there always? Strangely Elton John and Naomi Campbell have homes here, and they don't come across to me as people who like their privacy invaded in any way, but perhaps they change when here. And

Johnny Depp is rumoured to be buying a place here. It's an interesting city with a phenomenal history, but quirky with it. There is a street dedicated to a man who was a butcher and used the meat from babies. Of course he was executed, but they named a street after him.

I've had fish every meal, except breakfast. The restaurants are excellent. Paradiso 0415234910, Trattoria Alla Rivetta 041 5287302 and al Covo www.ristorantealcovo.com you need to book. They are the type of restaurants which film-makers invent because they don't exist in real life. They exist here although there is so much fairy-tale about Venice I'm not sure one could call living here 'real life'.

The Doge's Palace, from which we are five minutes walk, is beautiful and fascinating. Take a boat tour for an hour and get a very good overview of the city. You will quickly get an idea of where things are, something which seems impossible when you first arrive. I would highly recommend January in Venice. No crowds, the weather is interesting whether the light is bright and blue (was on our first day) or silver grey (as on our second), and you can easily spend hours in the restaurants, eating fresh seafood and teasing yourself with a Tiramisu if you must. And drink the hot chocolate. It is a must – even if you have to forgo one of the tours, drink the chocolate.

Plus points

It is a fairy tale adventure that is unique in the world. Catch it before it goes, and listen to the guides. The history is interesting on many levels. They were before their time, and still are.

Minus points

Expensive, and everyone is a merchant in Venice. The glass is lovely but doesn't travel well. And the smell and fog can be nauseating and annoying.

Interesting points

The Chinese tourists rampaging everywhere. They are like steam rollers. Watching the watchers as if they are about to create their own Venice in China. They do copy everything, after all,

HV – are you going to go?

Central location. Venice is a city built for walking, strolling, meandering, so choose a central base to make exploration easy. The extra cost is worth the experience of being in the heart and hub of the city.

LV – what may impact on your decision

The flooding which occurs at high tides, although that is part of the experience of Venice. The smell is however, quite strong, so take aromatherapy oils with you after the water has subsided. Small price to pay for such beauty.

Alternatives
There is none. That is why you should go. Venice is unique.

Possibilities
Very good destination for foodies. Our concierge asked what we preferred to eat, the price range, how far we would like to walk and what we were looking for (sophistication, character, authenticity) and then booked the table. You don't need to be knowledgeable about the restaurants, you just need to know what you like and how you like it. The concierge will do the rest. That is why it is imperative to choose your hotel well.

Choices
Go with a tour operator that knows their stuff. Choose a central location so you can walk easily everywhere. And breakfast and lunch like a king. Suppers are less important. Good place to wander around and must take a boat trip. .

TRAVEL WISDOM NUMBER THREE: TRAVEL MAKES YOU MORE PASSIONATE

I was doing a talk at a travel show about travel writing and a girl approached me at the end and asked how she could become 'passionate'. I could have said something trite like "meet the right guy" but it's very much an internal thing. I believe every woman is deeply passionate, and being more open to failure and success and 'taking both imposters just the same' she's more likely to be awakened by travelling. Every woman is Shirley Valentine, it's just that their 'wall' is usually their husband/partner/lover.

Suggested Journey: Buenos Aires

Buenos Aires is a fabulous wonderful exciting city. If Rome is the tease and Paris the foreplay, BA is the sex. It's sophisticated, earthy, intelligent, passionate, emotional, hot (over 40 degrees when I visited), unexpected, rebellious..and oh yes, it respects women and gives them space, and allows them to come first, when they want to.

In a powerfully feminine city, La Faena is the sexiest hotel in the world, like something from the future. Philippe Starck helped design the impressive hotel, which is in the heart of La Faena district. This area of the city has its own police force and is only reached by crossing a bridge.

They dance tango in the street, the men and women sticking to each other like glue. Turn meat-eater even if usually a vegetarian – the beef is like none other anywhere else in the world.

In my time in Buenos Aires I also stayed at Alvear Art Hotel (alveatart.com). on the way back from Antarctica (the ultimate male ego trip destination) and was given a tour of the city by the excellent guide Elizabeth Georges (elizabethgeorges@hotmail.com). I strongly recommend you hire her when you go there for the half or full day. After all the male testosterone puff-puff of male derring-do and conquest (both historically and on the ship), it was good to redress the balance. BA started to do that.

The Alvear Art Hotel is situated close to the colonial architecture of San Telmo to the Plaza de Mayo, where the Casa Rosada (Presidential Palace) is situated. It was from the balcony of the Casa Rosada that Eva Peron told her people to not cry for her.

The stories Elizabeth told were fascinating, but you will find none in the guidebook. There were armed police there with barricades waiting for the daily protests. When Eva died (her spirit much stronger than her body), the military took over, and the laws on abortion and divorce, which she had introduced during her reign, were revoked. Divorce only came back in the 1960s, legalised abortion never did.

Plus points

It will turn you into a vegetarian. After eating the beef here you won't touch the muck anywhere else in the world. It will teach you how to be sexy again. It will teach you the importance of colour. It will teach you why it's important to dance in the street when you want to, and be passionate about life.

Minus points

It is a tinder-box waiting to explode, politically and economically.

Interesting points

It is a city which celebrates women. They miss their Archbishop, who is now Pope. Eva Peron was before her time: the women there are intelligent and feisty and the men know it, fear it and respect it. If you are a woman travelling there alone you will love it.

HV – are you going to go?

Choose a central hotel so you can walk everywhere. Hire a one to one guide and you will get the most from your stay. Do not go on a group tour. Waste of money and you will get tired and bored quickly. Cost – book tickets well in advance. In BA, it's who you know and who knows who that matters. You get doors opened quickly.

LV – what may impact on your decision

Don't worry about the heat (good air conditioning everywhere) , the cost (you can eat and stay cheaply), the food (wonderful and variety) and the violence (travel intelligently and you will be fine).

Alternatives

Rio in Brazil: not as sophisticated although as sexy.

Possibilities

Often used as a gateway to South America. Stay for a week, you will want to stay two. Stay in two hotels – one bed and breakfast and one upmarket – in different parts of the city.

Choices

Breakfast and lunch like a king. Suppers are less important. And go to a dance club. Buy leather belts, and the gourd they have matcha tea in. And try the chocolate. Eat the chocolate.

TRAVEL WISDOM NUMBER FOUR: JOURNEYS GIVE CLARITY

Wilderness journeys are ideal for clearing the mind and for heartbreak. It's levelling to realise that what you most need in the world – in fact all you need in the world – is something to eat, somewhere warm to stay and something to drink. That's all you need – the rest is what you want. And a culture that thinks of romance in a completely different way also deals with heartbreak effectively. Go East.

Suggested journey: UK to China

Just back from China, which was fabulous. Tiananmen Square fascinating even without the tanks. The Great Wall was great, and old China still exists – the houtongs in Beijing and the French concession in Shanghai. My preference was Beijing. District 798 (which sounds like something out of Soylent Green) was wonderful, what Covent Garden would like to be, but a creative hub right in the heart of a city with 20 million population. Never did I feel crowded or suffocated, something I usually do when I go to central London. Phenomenal history. The Forbidden City, with its 8700-plus rooms plus, 24 Emperors, 3700 concubines, and approx 8-10000 population, left me awestruck.

The Great Wall is in fact a huge tomb, filled with the bodies of millions of slaves and prisoners who died building it. I'm told the crowd usually makes it a difficult trek, but if you join it at the right place you'll miss the traffic.You can go up by chair lift, down by toboggan, and still be able to bargain for chopsticks for a fraction of the price they were originally offered.

I tried fish lung soup and sea cucumber but not snake or dog. The dogs aren't scrawny things – they look unnervingly like the dog I'm looking after at the moment (Beethoven cute and gorgeous), but with more meat on. They tell you everything you eat makes you beautiful, strong and is brilliant for the skin so people eat it, even if it does taste and look odd. But the vegetable dumplings I tried in Shanghai were amazing.

Chinese food in China (as opposed to Chinese food I've tried at home) is some of the best food I've tried in the world. It's clever, not prissy and beautiful. Not as much ceremony as the Japanese nor as fragrant or subtle as the Thai, but clever. And they eat everything. My favourite is Indian food in India but I'd be happy to frog-hop from India to China and back again to sample some of their amazing ingredients.

My lasting impression: they like their power, they know how to get it, and learn fast. They will end up far better at capitalism than the West. But I hope they don't let go of the past. It's fascinating to visit.

Plus points
An interesting culture we can learn a lot from. Their history is phenomenal, surpassing even our own.

Minus points
There is none, it is just perspective.

Interesting points
They eat anything with four legs except a table. The pollution and traffic is not as bad as the media would have us believe.

HV – are you going to go?
Take three journeys to China, Beijing and Shanghai being one of them. Do not do the country in one go. It would be like trying to cram in Europe in three weeks.

LV – what may impact on your decision
You can't speak the language. It doesn't matter. It's part of the fun. It's the place most people say they want to visit and never do, so don't be one of them.

Alternatives
There is none. That is why you should go.

Possibilities

Day trip from Hong Kong, but it's a bit like a day trip anywhere. You won't really see it.

Choices

Choose a one-on-one guide while you're there so you don't waste time or money.

TRAVEL WISDOM NUMBER FIVE: JOURNEYS COMBAT LONELINESS

You can be lonely in a crowd, if it's the wrong crowd. You can be lonely with your partner, if it's the wrong partner.

If you feel alone, go on your journey by yourself. You are never alone, not really. Being 'lonely' is essentially not being happy with yourself, your opinions, your belief, your feelings, your values. Feeling lonely is feeling lost. We are a composite of our experiences. We gain better sense of self and worth when travelling than standing still. That's why teenagers, especially, benefit from travel during a time of unprecedented physical, mental, emotional and hormonal change.

Suggested Journey: The Yukon

I am traveling to the Yukon for nine days, taking a journey with my son Tom, that I took fifteen years ago for the Discovery Channel. Then I had a film crew in tow and was four months pregnant (they didn't know that at the time, but the makeup artist looked into my eyes and asked if I was pregnant – you can tell by the eyes) and I had to sign documents to say that it was my responsibility etc. But Tom benefitted from the adventure in my tummy, and now he's going to benefit from it as a teenager.

I am, however, going to be driving an RV. I've never driven an RV before, and I should imagine it's a bit like a tank but with hot and cold running water, better facilities, and more space. Thankfully the roads in the Yukon are wide and open and the scenery is quite simply the most stunning I have ever seen in all my travels. It leaves you breathless.

I remember meeting park rangers, and talking bear encounters with locals who had defended themselves with the use of pepper spray and little dogs (the smaller the better) and meeting a gold-miner who asked if I would be his wife, which was rather sweet, if inappropriate. I met some people from the First Nations who told me Tom's spiritual animal would be an eagle and he would 'fly' in life, which he's certainly done a lot of over the years in our travels (I think they meant in other ways too…). I kayaked through lakes past icebergs, had a bath in an old freezer box looking out at said iceberg lake, and did this all on camera. I danced with the dancers in the theatre in Dawson City, fished in the lakes, hiked the chilkoot trail and encountered and ate moose. I tried to kill a wild salmon with the back of an axe (for TV they like it dramatic, if improbable), and managed to give the poor thing concussion. I eventually did it, third take; I still live with the guilt.

Oh yes, and listened to an actor reciting the poems of Robert Service, the bard of the Yukon (though he was Scottish). The actor stood in the wilderness in an outdoor theatre and recited one poem 'The Quitter', which is about never giving up or giving in, something my father use to say to me all the time. As he'd recently died, it made me very emotional, but despite the director's request to have tears on camera, I told him a categorical no. Think this trip will be emotional too. Driving the RV is the least of it.

The Yukon is the most awe-inspiring place in the world. The scenery is jaw-droppingly spectacular but I am driving an RV so my first day was spent being glued to the screen looking at the road. Screw the scenery, I don't want to crash.

I am relaxing into it, which may be a good sign. I did this with my ex's Lotus and I killed it swerving to miss a rabbit. But they have great big ruddy moose out here so I have an excuse this time.

Yesterday we hiked with our excellent guide Brent to Kathleen Lake. We saw lots of bear droppings but no bear. They like snowberries so lots of snowberry 'pies' on the trail.

Kathleen Lake itself is incredible, teeming with fish so the bears here are very happy. The greatest lakes are always the ones named after women. They are the most beautiful, the most serene and wondrous, but become dangerous and treacherous at a moment's breath. Not fair and not true. But 'she' was stunning.

We then took a small plane and flew over the glacier at Kluane National Park. The glacier looks prehistoric and terrifying. We flew over the iceberg lakes I kayaked through fifteen years ago when I was pregnant with Tom. The guides we had then were incredible. Strong, suppportive, grounded. I remember them as distinctly as I do the journey itself. Daniel carefully explained the names of the mountains and rivers as we flew over them. Many were named by the First Nation Indians who gave each one a poetic name such as 'Whispering Bear' or 'Laughing Eagle." And what did the goldminers call them? Disenchantment River and Disappointment Mountain. Typical. I think they should call one 'Hiccuping Chipmunk' as there are so many round here, and they are so cute. But alas, I ran one over one.

Everyone has a bear story to tell. There was the story about the man who walked along the path and found a fully grown grizzly bearlying still. As the man drew closer he realised the bear wasn't sleeping, but was dead. They later found out that there was moose calf in the bear's stomach and two large moose hoof-prints on the bear. The mother had killed it, obviously annoyed the bear had eaten its calf. Then there was the one about the little terrier called Charlie who frightened a full grown grizzly away. Everyone tells that story, only the name of the dog changes.

We haven't seen a bear. We're still on our bear hunt, but the scenery has been spectacular. The roads are either wonderful or extremely bumpy. The views blisteringly beautiful. Soppy thing that I am, I have been in tears. Tom has managed to tear himself away from the ipad. We are going over the top of the world today, which even I think sounds cool. Watched a vaudeville show last night in Beaver Creek. Lots of Americans, two Canadians and us. Everyone asked if we liked the baby names. (I presumed they referred to Kate's baby). Completely different world. I didn't care.

I haven't been eaten by bears. Mosquitoes yes, but not bears.

I have covered a lot of miles. Almost as many as they do in the Yukon Quest (1000) albeit not with huskies in minus 50, just an RV that hopefully will bring us back in one piece.

My itinerary is bonkers, so although I'm a free spirit and this is the land of the free spirit I'm up against time all the time and looking to see if I've run out of diesel so I don't feel very free. I feel very stressed. It doesn't help that some of the signs are in miles, others are in kilometers, and some are both. Passed through Beaver Creek, although didn't see any beavers – or bears – and crossed into Alaska. Border control is always interesting into the States. I always get the impression they don't want you in their country, no matter how many 'have a nice days' I hear thereafter. First impressions matter. First stop is Chicken, a small place where all the souvenirs revolve around the slogan 'I got laid in...Chicken'. Yup.

The Top of the World road is stunning. Again no bears, but a tour bus on its side in the mud. In the absence of taking a photo of the bears, I took a picture of it.

Dawson City I remember well from my last trip. Little has changed. It's got a bit bigger but the tour around Dredge Four and the Gold Bottom mining tour are fascinating. And we found gold – all $7 worth of it.

Then a 400 mile drive to Tombstone Park. Shattered. Still no bears. But the best day so far was with the Cathers in Lake Laberge. An incredible family with so many stories – bear and otherwise – I could have stayed there all week. They teach you how to sledge with huskies, but they do it properly in the most stunning setting. You can hike with them and go canoeing in the lake, which is beautiful, but in my articles I'll write more about the stories. Some of them involve people pissing up trees, sliding along ice at 20mph trying to correct huskies going in the wrong direction, and playing chicken with black bears.

Then met Keith Wolf Smarch, who taught Tom how to gut fish he'd just caught. He's a master wood carver and taught Tom how to carve. Tom helped with a totem pole. Now that's something he can put on his CV. "I helped carve a totem pole'. There's experiential travel for you!

Plus points

A wilderness experience that takes you out of yourself and your ego. Yukoners are laid back, speak English, and like the English.

Minus points

It is expensive to get from A to B. You're focusing on the amount of diesel you have in the engine – even free spirits need diesel. You need to be 'awake' all the time as this is the wilderness. You aren't in a zoo. You are surrounded by wild animals who don't come out when you want them to and don't disappear when you'd like them to.

Interesting points

The history of this place is fascinating and curiously relevant. It's about the iconic journeys of people who went in search of 'gold' and found the wealth in the landscape but also in how the landscape pushed them to greater challenges and strengthened them as people. They found their wealth in the strength of personality.

Alternatives

Wilderness adventure from the outback of Australia, to trekking through the Amazon, to mountain biking in Skye, to the Highlands of Scotland

Choices

Are you going to rough it? RV? Four Wheel Drive? By foot? Duration?

TRAVEL WISDOM NUMBER SIX: JOURNEYS COMBAT ANGER

Anger is an emotion that emanates from fear. All negative energies, anger, and hatred derive from fear. Confronting fear, we confront anger. Journeys to take when feeling angry are those which are 'bigger' than you. For example, the Grand Canyon literally absorbs the energy, swallowing it up. It can take it.

Women are angry, but it's interpreted as fear. Men are afraid, but it's interpreted as anger. Women cry when they are angry. Men get angry when they are afraid. Anger comes from fear. Confront the fear, you confront the anger, and where there is no room for fear there is no room for anger.

"Confronting your fears, whatever they are, is the way forward. On a journey where there are continual challenges, there is no room to feel self-pity. The key is to keep the energy to yourself, the knowledge to yourself. Tell yourself you have done well, but keep the experience to yourself. Don't shout about it." Dan Snow.

Suggested Journey: The Grand Canyon

The Canyon swallows up all thought like some emotional vacuum. It is simply too vast and overwhelmingly beautiful to take in, which is why so many visitors burst spontaneously into tears. As I did. All it would have taken to have me sobbing uncontrollably was Barber's *Adagio for Strings*. There are many moments like this over the next 24 hours.

Neither word nor image can do justice to something that simply defies definition. Gradually it strikes me how the place is full of people staring into the deep, wrinkled distance: men and women lost in the moment, looking for the meaning of life. Or just the meaning of theirs.

Plus points

Accessible as part of a much larger trip through California and Nevada. Walking tours, camping trips, kayaking and hiking.

Minus points

Increasingly touristy, which disrupts the energy while there.

Interesting points

The trip initially uses the energy of anger/aggression in a constructive way. Aggression used in a positive way drives people forward; in a negative way – without activity – it holds people back. Walking up and down the Canyon or taking a longer trek of any sort with an ultimate goal uses the aggression and focuses the mind so that, rather than ignoring it, the journey uses the energy to move forward.

Alternatives

Base Camp of Everest. Climbing Kilimanjaro. Trekking through Nepal or Bhutan where the culture is gentle and those who live there, live in the moment, not for the future or the past.

Choices

A long weekend or a two-week break – or a month-long trek? How much anger do you have? Once you're progressing on from the initial emotion, you're identifying how to deal with it in future, what triggers it in you, and how you can focus it in another way.

"Physically, a hike or climb in the mountains of the UAE or Oman, where I spend 6 months a year, or a run in the New Forest, my UK home, will invariably pick me up, And outside of this, there are a number of countries in the world that have an energy that is palpable, such as Nepal, Bali, Bhutan or Thailand. I guess it's no coincidence that they are Buddhist or Hindu cultures, both of which give a very positive energy and vibe."

– Adrian Hayes, explorer

TRAVEL WISDOM NUMBER SEVEN: JOURNEYS CAN HELP YOU BOND WITH YOUR TEENAGER

Places to take your teenager – Las Vegas.

You have not failed as a mother if your teenager enjoys a place associated with debauched Princes, pathologically unfaithful celebrities and gambling losers. It is a city of lights in the middle of a desert and has shows which deserve the description *spectacular*. Teenagers are not allowed to gamble here, thank goodness, nor can they come within a hundred yards of alcohol. This means you will need to do the same and tame your choice of show.

Suggested Journey: California-Nevada Loop

This trip includes flying to LA, driving along the coast to San Francisco, then onto Yosemite, Death Valley, Las Vegas, Grand Canyon, Lake Havasu and Joshua Tree National Park before returning to LA. It's a trip with incredible variety, best taken with a group in a VW camper van or with your teenager, who will be aware and appreciative of things you are not. For example, Alcatraz (book a month or two in advance if travelling in the summer) has a fascinating and gruesome history. The wine region will leave them cold, while the temperatures in the summer in San Francisco resemble those of an English summer, so be aware. Temperature goes up again once you reach Yosemite, which has incredible rock climbing, rafting, hiking and tree-hugging opportunities.

Death Valley, the next stop on route, is a madly undersold destination you must stop at, but never break down in, as temperatures regularly reach over fifty degrees centigrade (hot oven). This is a National Park and hence the guides – full of knowledge and passion and that rare quality, an ability to impart information with enthusiasm without jargon – are a find in themselves. I met one who was seventy-five and wouldn't work anywhere else. Ironically he had never felt more alive than in 'Death Valley'.

Las Vegas, the original sin city, transforming its image from decadent gambling capital of the world to clubbing big show capital of the world, still has the sex shows, the seediness without looking too hard or fast, but it takes a teenager to see the wow in this city of lights in the middle of a desert. There are shows that don't have tits and bums in them. You don't need to buy anything in the Malls; people watching and the shows they put on are entertainment enough. In the old part of the Vegas, the light show performed to Queen's 'We Will Rock You' always succeeds in doing just that. It's bubblegum culture at it's very best and although you won't want a lot of it, one bite is enough. You need a taste, nothing more and the road trip – stopping off at Vegas but not staying there, satisfies the appetite.

The Canyon, on the other hand is an early morning excursion. You need to rise at five to see anything of the Canyon, to get down and up before nine when the temperatures rise into their nineties. Watch the light dancing on the rocks, the goats sticking like glue to near vertical slopes, and people on horses wishing they had chosen to walk as riding has made it an even longer fall.

Lake Havasu belongs to a surrealist painting, not real life. London Bridge, a simple brick bridge, in the middle of middle America, in sweltering heat and wide roads with condos, looks out of place. Camp by the Lake at the excellent campsite and consider the madness that works in a country where anything is possible, even the impossible. The journey is the ultimate in 'can do'.

And Joshua Tree National Park, each tree pointing you onward to LA, and Santa Monica and the yoga studios and breakfast bars that do amazing things with scrambled eggs and omelette with every conceivable egg-laying animal going.

Plus points
Offers a variety. Something for everyone. Someone else does the driving if going with a tour operator.

Minus points
Don't spend too much time in the van or car. Dull and restrictive. In and out all the time, camping, packing and unpacking. Keep it short. No more than ten days.

Interesting points
Las Vegas is surprisingly good for teenagers. It focuses adults on what the place has to offer that isn't gambling or about sex or clubbing. It is a city of lights in the middle of a desert. That's an amazing phenomenon.

Alternatives
Train through Europe, stopping off at the major cities. Wonderful way to see the country. Choose central hotels from which it is easiest to reach the

main attractions. This also offers variety and ease of travel.

Choices
Identify what you want the outcome of the trip to be.

SIX: THE TRAVEL ALPHABET

"Food becomes important when you don't have it. Water becomes important when you don't have it. Warmth becomes important when you don't have it. It's not until you are in this position you realise just how important these things are. I'd say that was the most fundamental journey of discovery, wouldn't you?"
Bear Grylls.

Travel writers tend to focus on the where to go and what to do. Here is an A to Z of thoughts and feelings to consider when travelling. It is a guideline to show how to think about travel in a different way, to observe. It doesn't tell you how to think or what to think, just shows you how I've done it over the past twenty years.

Where to begin?

For all those who want to write a book or believe they have a book inside them, not knowing where to start is the excuse they give for not starting their book. The same goes for a journey. So do you begin with a round the world trip, to be completed within a certain time frame to then re enter life back home and get what your parents tell you is a 'real job?. I've met many of these gap travellers, not all innocent know-it-all students, but mid life crisis 30- or 40-somethings, who realise their real job is just an illusion of security, keeping them locked into fears they shed when they travel.

The round-the-worlders tend to stop off in a destination, meet and marry a love, have a family and not continue on their journey, if ever. Canada has a culture and value set not dissimilar to the British. Their winters are foul, they have dissension in Quebec as we do in Scotland, but Canadians are essentially at peace with themselves as we are in the UK. Everything is relative.

Eat Pray Love espoused the myth of traveling to find yourself, your spirituality, your love of life, your sense of humour and sense of perspective, sense of self, sense of self reliance, your *sense*. Choosing destinations which enable you to 'find yourself' – your soul and spirit, bashed down by the minutia and trivialities of life such as mortgage, schooling of children, paying of bills – is something everyone thinks about on holiday and then forgets as soon as back home in the swing of the everyday.

This is a pity. We make such big dreams when on holiday and when traveling. We're going to leave that job, tell that boss where to go, take that RV around

California, Harley Davidson Route 66, train it round Europe. Go on that safari. Work in Australia for a year – or try to. Do David Attenborough but without the cameras. We think the big picture (see B, big picture) and what is important, really important, comes to the foreground.

So think about this. Think about this moment. You are on your death bed. You know you are about to die. That's it. Life as you know it in this body is over. What are you going to regret? You are going to regret what you haven't done, rather than what you have done. I promise you that. And you will regret not having travelled with all your heart, and all your soul and all your mind. Think about that the next time you get the chance to travel.

A

Adventure

The definition of adventure is like the definition of success: it differs for everyone. To some it is moving to another village or town or part of the country. To others it is scaling the heights of Mount Everest, to others still it is conquering their own fears, which may seem slight to others but have grown to mean something much deeper and darker to them.

To me adventure means pushing boundaries – my boundaries, not the official boundaries. It means breaking through long established-fears of failing, or proving to myself (not anyone else) that I can do something.

My greatest adventures are skydiving, mountain climbing, bungee-jumping, aerobatic flying, kite-surfing, swimming with dolphins, stingrays, seals, and whales, and Antarctic iceberg walking,

Advertising

The countries with the biggest PR budgets get the biggest shout. This does not mean they are the most interesting destinations or have the most to offer. They just have the best PR,

Ageing

Travel and ageing is an interesting one. Apart from time travel, all travel according to experts is technically ageing as ageing is caused by stress amongst other things, and travel can be stressful. Of course there's an increase in spas and health resorts which focus on anti ageing the skin which may have been aged in the process of getting there. There are also locations where the air (mountain air famously clean) and natural moisture in the air (Far East where there is predominantly wet heat as opposed to dry) renders walking outside equivalent to a steam room which is according to Antonia Mariconda, skin expert, extremely good for the pores and delays the ageing process. Other ageing culprits when you travel include sun exposure, smoking (don't travel with a smoker), pollution, chronic stress, poor sleeping, diet and exercise habits. It may be reassuring for those who don't exercise to know that if you exercise too much it is also ageing (activates free radicals), so smug marathon runners beware. So basically any sort of family holiday, and city break is out. And travelling with anyone who might stress you out. So you may return feeling younger but may in fact, look older.

Astrology

Countries and cities have birthdays too according to Sharon Burbidge, psychic astrologer which means they have star signs. If the country or city is your star sign this does not necessarily mean you will like the place (just as you may not like someone of your own sign in real life). London is Gemini, (fast, communicative, multi faceted) but then again so are many other cities round the world, which have different star signs. And Libra seems to have captured all the places I personally love (Argentina, Canada, China, Tibet) and Leo has France and Italy to themselves. "Its to do with the elements – earth, fire, air, water. If you're a water sign you'll like to be by water – rivers, oceans, if you are air, you'll like mountains and the cold, fire, hot, dry and arid climates, and earth is countryside, valleys, walking." She tells me. Personally I'm not sure. If it were true, I'm a little bit of everything.

B

'Be'

"I see guests come off the plane," a woman looking after a villa rental in Sardinia told me this year, "and more and more they walk though the gates in a thoroughly dazed state of stress. Professional couples and families, but all they want to do is lie by the pool read and sleep. Even five years ago, they would have been hiking, riding, trekking, travelling all over the place. Now they just want to 'be'".

We are a nation of stressed-out individuals finding it harder to chill out each year, but we also think that we know it all already. We've read about it, watched it on TV and talked to those who've had the full experience. So why bother to explore at all? To learn about ourselves.

Beach Etiquette

Work this one out. Every week, at my local gym, I observe a sea of men and women with their personal trainers, pedalling, spinning and kickboxing their way to a peak of physical perfection. Yet whenever I find myself on the beach in the South of France, I never see these toned folk at all. Perhaps it's because they all have their own holiday homes, or even – knowing the clientele at this club – their own private sand plage.

Even so, no matter where I am, I can always spot the Englishman on a beach. Whatever the weather – rain, wind, hail or heat – he will be out in it, fighting them on the beaches with a grim determination that would make Winston Churchill proud.

Admittedly we Brits see the sun less often than most, which may account for our excess of adulation when we do. I remember once visiting Turkey when it was so hot – think oven on a regulo plenty – that the government closed all its offices for a week and innumerable offices for a week and innumerable chickens died. Whether the second event was directly consequential upon the first is anyone's guess. Either way, while fowl and bureaucrat floundered, the nutty English struggled on, baking, burning and dehydrating in their own inimitable way. The results were unedifying in the extreme – a beach is one place where few people look prettier in pink.

Another sure sign of an Englishman on the beach is the noise. The art of gliding silently across the sand with minimal fuss, exuding confidence and stealth, has yet to establish itself in the standard Anglo-Saxon repertoire. Especially not in the case of short people, who – for some curious evolutionary reason – invariably have the loudest voice. I may be lying at the other end of the Cap D'Antibes, but it if my fellow beach dwellers are English and under five foot five, I will still be able to get the low down on Heather's hysterectomy or Tracy's stunning GCSEs.

Furthermore, the English almost all behave as though they've never previously encountered sand.

Apparently fearful of being sucked in by this alien substance, they tiptoe tentatively across the strand to the most inconspicuous spot they can find – unless, of course, they are short, in which case the very concept of lying low in about as appealing as prohibition to a brewer.

Yet despite the English beach preference for avoiding the limelight, we invariably choose a spot with a good view of everyone else. To the English a beach is essentially a widescreen TV for which the licence comes free of charge. We are a nation of beach voyeurs, watching furtively as those of less decorous stock have their uninhibited fun I the sun.

And why not? On the beach, there is plenty to see – and, in certain countries, much of it is legalised porn. For me, the world's best 'body watching' beaches are in Brazil, closely followed by those in Sydney, where bikinis and trunks leave just enough for the imagination, and where the concept of a beach bum takes on a whole different slant. And then there's California, from which I've just returned. This too is replete with the boned and the toned.

As for nudist beaches, you won't find the best bodies here, but you will see more of them. Furthermore, everyone is very polite and deeply aware of personal space. No one looks intently at anyone else. In fact, by a none –too gentle irony, nudist beaches provide the ultimate proof of what every red-blooded man and woman instinctively knows that wearing a little something is infinitely sexier than pitching up in nothing at all.

So if you're thinking of baring all on the beach this summer, don't be temped to have a peek in the neighbouring dune. Take a good book instead. I wouldn't dream of manipulating you but as it happens, I can thoroughly recommend my own.

Plan B – master of disasters.

What if the plane doesn't take off on time? What happens if we miss our connection? What happens if it rains? What happens if there isn't a doctor near by? Something else happens. If we worried all the time about the *what if*s in life we wouldn't get out of bed in the morning. Prepare for what ifs with a Plan B and C and D, but don't let it stop you from the possibility of Plan A working.

C

Conflict

To travel hopefully, as Robert Louis Stevenson observed, is often more important than to arrive. But when it comes to those precious annual holidays, whom you choose to travel with could be the most important issue of all.

We've all been there. A friendship fashioned hastily in the playground, office, pub or gym falls flat within a week, as a shared Cotswolds cottage or Spanish villa turns rapidly into a prison without bars.

The key to understanding the problem is to grasp the fact that much of life is based on illusion. School gate and dinner-party friendships are not real, as they are lightly forged through brief and intermittent meetings during which everyone is on best behaviour. That may be fine for a few hours – keeping it up for a fortnight is a different game again. Playground alliances can quickly turn to poison: more than one family of my acquaintance has ended up moving the children to another school following an unsuccessful shared family break.

If you do decide to share your holiday, be sure to manage your expectations. Different families have different parenting values – some parents are keen to spend time with their children, others want to sign them up for a kids club. Discipline is also an issue: you may be able to keep your own brood in line, but what happens when les petits cheris of the other couple are allowed to run riot?

Then there's the money. This too can be the root of all kinds of evil, as not everyone has the same budget. One family has season tickets for Maxim's; another prefers self-catering with two plates and a pot. Wand what about the hours you keep? Owls may go to sea with pussycats, but when they set sail with larks at the ship is generally destined for the rocks. If rising at dawn for a hike along the cliffs is your thing, there's no point in vacationing with all-night clubbers who rarely make it up before lunch. It may sound like basic common sense, but you'd be amazed how many people ignore it.

Even being with those you know and love best can have its problems. Many families now boast two working parents who see little of their children – and each other – during the week. Some regard this as s necessary evil, but others thrive on it. One man even told me that not seeing his children had helped him to become a better father. And if that's how he felt about his own crew, imagine the fireworks if he were forced to play happy campers with someone else's.

Throw in the politics of divorce, and the minefield is just about complete. When I split from my husband I arranged for three families to stay at different times with my son and me at our home in France. The first two visits worked like a dream, but the third – from a family consisting of husband, wife and four children – was a disaster. The couple were mutual friends of my ex husband and myself, and consequently I was never sure whether any of what I said would be relayed back to the ex with whom, as it happens, I was not on speaking terms. The woman had also invited her parents to stay nearby, so we were soon outnumbered eight to two.

It was overwhelming, especially as my son didn't get on with their four. The final straw was when a good friend of mine flew down for a long weekend and one of the four kids continually interrupted our conversation. I asked her to stop. Big mistake. As her mother later tactfully explained, they had only agreed to stay because they felt sorry for me, and thus I should have been grateful that they were there at all. Now my ex isn't the only one I don't talk to.

Of course, there are times when it all works out. Friends from school or college, for example, are usually a good bet as holiday companions. The two of you have a shared history and long-established mutual affection, so even the most outrageous fortune is unlikely to pull you apart. Activity breaks are also fertile ground for sharing, as the activity itself provides a focus on which everyone can agree. Climbing in the Alps, riding boogying in Barcelona – each forms a logical extension to something which you already enjoy at home.

But these are breaks for individuals. When it comes to sharing a family holiday with another family, my advice, on the whole is don't, there are simply too many variables. In the adult world one compromises virtually all the time. If you end up having to do it on holiday, you may be better off on your own.

Creativity

Some journeys instigate it and some waste it. What makes you creative? Have you ever thought about that? What fires you into thinking laterally? Is it a mind-mapping exercise where you go to unexpected places in your head? Places also do that. They challenge you to think in a different way, behave in a different way, speak in a different way. Most of us lead such little lives, and the idea of leaving the norm, the safety of repetition, scares us. But it is this moving out of the comfort zone that ignites creativity. It is stagnation that kills it. It is sitting still that kills it.

Cultures

Some cultures appear very rude. It's just the way it is. I can't mention which ones because that would be un-PC, but even the language of some cultures can sound aggressive, even when the meaning behind it is not. Some languages have a gentle assonance that makes every syllable sound like a lullaby.

There are countries where women are looked down on. In fact, there are a lot of countries women are looked down on, some are more obvious than others, but even in the western world, many countries still treat women like second class citizens. Ladies, take it in your stride. It is their stuff not yours, so whether you call it culture or ignorance, it doesn't belong to you, it belongs to them. You don't need to respect or buy into it or challenge it, your purpose is to observe it, just as you would a penguin on an iceberg. Fascinating to watch, but not of your world.

Celebrity travel

It's been said many times before, but celebrities are the high priests of the age. Every aspect of their lives – from their mansions to their makeup – is treated as a holy relic, an object of veneration for a secular world.

And nothing fascinated us more than knowing where these fantasy folk chill out. Reams of paper – a veritable rainforest of trivia – are taken up in the publication of articles about their holiday hideaways, while B list celebs are wheeled out to present TV travel shows, as though their expertise in modelling or rapping made them arbiters of aesthetic taste.

Hotels, however display a somewhat ambiguous attitude towards the patronage of their celebrity guests. Frequently they treat the famous much as they would a ghost: aware of an invisible presence, yet behaving for all practical purposes as though the person did not exist. Hotels boasting the genuine article – A-listers – prefer to keep quiet about it for fear of driving them away. Only those obliged to settle for the supporting cast parade their insecurity by shouting out the script, often in exaggerated form.

As a general rule, I have some simple advice for anyone tempted to choose a holiday haven on the baissi of its glitzy clientele: don't do it. For a start, top-flight celebrities pay the hotel to keep the hidden, so if you're planning to spend a fortnight celebrity-spotting, you're in for a tedious time. You might as well go looking for a penguins in a desert as wait for Brad Pitt to come strolling into the lobby with a beach ball.

Secondly hotels that cater for celebrities will invariably – though not exclusively – attract a rum selection of spoilt pampered types who will do nothing for your holiday mood. Think Amy Winehouse without the talent, and you're close.

Thirdly, just because the hotels looks after celebrities well, it doesn't mean that it's going to accord you the same level of care and attention. An ugly truth, but a truth nonetheless.

And finally – for those who hadn't already worked this out – the cost of staying at such a hotel won't be anyone's idea of a bargain. Owing to their status and contacts, few celebrities will be paying their own way – even though they could well afford to do so. In your case I'm guessing that the hotline to the Hilton is continually on hold, so expect to see your wallet empty faster than a pub with no beer. Ten yeas ago, I produced and presented a series on Sky called Who's *been sleeping in my bed*? in which I interviewed the great and the good in their favourite hotels around the world. Sir David Frost for example, chose Chewton Glen in the New Forest while the late Anita Roddick and Lord Yehudi Menuhin both plumbed for L'Amigo in Brussels where they had stayed on visits to the United Nations.

It was a fascinating series to produce learning that the model Marie Helvin always took her owns sheets and pillow whereever she went and than Menuhin became cross whenever hotels offered him a small room just because he was a very small man.

But my clearest recollection that most of those I met simply wanted to be treated like everyone else. Or so they told me in haste. However, if they were ever actually to experience the way the rest of us are treated in some of the celebrity hotels, they would quickly repent at their leisure.

Courage

Think of the great explorers. Go buy the books and read their adventures and what it took for them to achieve what they did. It will put your own journeys into perspective. When I travelled to the Antarctic, I learnt how those before had travelled using everything they could, failing time after time, – trying dogs, mules, motorbikes and tractors. They pushed themselves. Push yourself. It awakens the spirit and enriches the soul.

Children

I like my own. I love my own. I like other children when they are polite and funny and kind. You don't need to like other peoples'. It doesn't make you a bad person if you don't like children, as long as you love your own. So choose wisely when travelling to a 'family friendly' resort. You will be surrounded by them.

As someone who has written about traveling with children over the past twenty years, and having traveled with my son since he was a babe in arms, I have found certain cultures to be far more friendly and relaxed with our children than we are. Countries such as Portugal, Spain, Greece, even Denmark are more child-centric than our own culture which merely tolerates them and puts a 'family friendly' on hotel and restaurant signs as if it's an added bonus rather than innate to our culture. Dr Rachel claims "How cultures react to children and animals says a lot about how they react to emotion. The compassion we show to those who are most vulnerable – that is children and animals – mirrors the compassion we show to the vulnerability in ourselves. Travel only broadens the mind that is willing to learn and when we are at our most vulnerable; full of fear, hatred, grief, sadness, anger – in short, full of emotion we are unable to control – then we are at most open to change and growth."

Character

Think of countries in terms of being people. The USA for example. If the USA were a person it would be a self-obsessed neurotic with obsessive, compulsive disorder, but with days of brilliance. Larger than life, one gets a glimpse of its scale, its beauty, its drama and its people through film – but you've got to be there to capture the energy which is relentless. The USA is as diverse in its geography as it is in its cultures, politics, values. New York is fast, edgy, gritty, funny, clever, can-do, with substance and style. LA is needy, shallow, superficial, open, wannabee with some style, little substance. Both have their seedy sides that they don't want to expose least of all to themselves. If you drive a Harley from east to west coast along the no-longer-completely -in-existence Route 66, the impression you'll get of the continent is that there are a lot of churches and a lot of sex shops. That quote came from a fourteen-year old.

America is all show, all about the business of show, but it puts on a phenomenal show. The Canyon will leave you gazing into the abyss searching for the meaning of your life, rather than life; Vegas will make you high, then drop you, Death Valley will haunt you, and Yosemite and any of the National Parks will never leave you, because you won't want to leave them. New York has the largest sweet and toy shop in the world. Live in the moment, because in the USA everything goes so fast, every moment is different. It's difficult not to be perceived as laid-back and understated, but Canada by comparison is so laid-back it's positively horizontal. Especially compared to the USA.

That said, Canadians will always tell you there are more bald eagles in Canada than there are in the USA, so they know where is best..

Cinema Paradiso

The kisses at the end – don't cut out all the best bits. Don't lose the soul and purpose of the trip. Lose sight of what you want to achieve, get distracted. And remember the first time (see F Firsts), the first romance when you travel. Write about it and look back on it wistfully, with affection. It will never happen again that way with that intention.

D

Death

Death, bereavement, and separation kick-start you into action. These are definitive journeys that will do it without the trauma, or help you through a trauma. And make you smile. So, whatever you want to do, do it. There are only so many tomorrows. Go find yourself. It will leave you speechless in awe, and then turn you into a storyteller of your own journey rather than reading about someone else's.

Danger

It may not be the Black Death exactly, but every outbreak of swine flu, bird flu, or any type of flu transmitted by animals to humans is a timely reminder that, if you travel to the ends of the Earth, there's always a chance that you'll come back with more than just a stick of rock. Many an email have I received from the Foreign Office, updating the list of no-go areas that tourists are urged to avoid. Natural disasters and political unrest are the prime offenders, but when a possible pandemic appears to be taking root, there is only one sensible course of action for those intent on visiting the source – don't.

Not that everyone listens. Whatever the advice emanating from Whitehall, there are those who will always dive into danger, compelled to free themselves from their comfort zones for the next 'tick box' traveller's tale. I once attended a dinner party at which a guy talked endlessly about his passion for climbing mountains,. Great big mountains that no one had ever heard of (I certainly hadn't), but that were even more dangerous and demanding than Everest – which, needless to say, our fearless friend was due to tackle the following spring.

Without wishing to make molehills of his mountains, I couldn't help asking why he chose to push himself in quite such an insouciant way. He was, after all, a family man with four children. His reply was that life is short, and that he wanted to spend his hour upon the stage feeling 'alive' rather than yield to the monotony of the domestic routine. This, apparently, necessitated the serial ascent of lethal summits, in flagrant disregard of the socking great drops on either side.

Personally I thought he was a selfish, boorish little boy. Yet my opinion was not generally shared. Before one could say Khyber Pass, the entire table was absorbed in a bewildering game of one-upmanship, as diners eagerly swapped holiday tales of the times when they felt most 'naive'.

Then there were the close encounters with the locals: the stories of being mugged, nearly being mugged or – in the case of one real boy scout – mugging the hapless mugger back. Unsurprisingly, this guy was a City bond trader. All it needed was for someone to say that they had actually been killed in the mugging and were really only present in spirit.

But there is a serious point here. Somewhere between the futile bravado of these reckless adventurers and the undue caution which would keep us all permanently in bed, shivering for fear of the swine flue, is a disconcertingly hazy middle ground. It may have been no-go-Mexico this month, but where do you draw the line in steering clear of risk? Is a civil war always a good reason to stay away? Or a soaring crime rate? Or even an infestation of tsetse fly?

Well, for guidance, the Foreign Office website (www.fco.gov.uk) is an excellent first port of call, with its up to date list of place to avoid, along with the reasons for doing so.

There are no guarantees – even in the safest places, where every crime is viewed as a serious affair. In Monte Carlo they arrest camera crews who have no permit; in Singapore one can be apprehended for spitting gin in public, and in Marrakesh, the old 'Red City' of Morocco, thieves who steal from tourists can expect to lose their hands. Yet even here there will always be the odd opportunist. For some people reward looms larger than risk. Just ask my mountain man and his friends.

E

Eco-anything

I've always been wary of anything with 'eco' in front of its name. The implication, it seems to me, is that the brand, or policy, or whatever, is somehow exempt from criticism, soaring above suspicion in the company of Caesar's wife. Rather like cyclists, in fact.

Eco is the place where worthy and bland converge. Just as rice cake is supposedly good for you, but tasteless wihtout a whole lot of bad stuff on top, so the ecosphere is the unsugared pill of rectitude; subliminally high church and self-consciously holier-than-thou. Eco-friendly, eco-lodge, eco-nomic: I mistrust it all.

Nor is the travel industry immune. Eco-tourism has traditionally beenn a bit like the health food section of a supermarket: specialist, slightly more expensive and trying hard to infiltrate the other brands.

Not that its advocates would put it quite like that. According to Simon Beeching, founder of sustainability strategy consultancy Travelwatch Ltd, ecotourism is all about 'finding a sustainable balance between tourism and the husbandry of the local resources and respect for local social needs". And the approach is catching on. Once the preserve of the open-toed-sandal brigade, it has now been adopted by many smaller travel companies with strong ties to the destinations they serve, as well as featuring increasingly on the agenda of travel associations and conglomerates, such as ABTA and TUI.

Furthermore the research I carried out for my book on travelling with teenagers suggests that the next generation – those classified as Generation Z (born after 1990) – is far more environmentally and globally aware than that of its parents. The eco-friendly message may not have quite got through to us, but it has certainly got through to our kids.

Time, I decided, to take it all a bit more seriously, to don my responsible hat and sift through the merits and demerits of the eco-realm. And Tom's Eco Lodge on the Isle of Wight looked like the ideal place to do it.

A short drive from the lovely ferry port of Yarmouth, it's a working dairy farm attached to a manor house, which guests can rent out in entirety. The actual eco-lodges are set out far from the sea, with cows roaming around and an area where hens run free. Each morning or afternoon you can collect your own free range eggs – provided, of course, that the families in the other lodges are unencumbered by overzealous seven-year-old with propensity for grabbing all the eggs themselves.

Milking takes place at 4am and 4pm, to appropriate musical accompaniment: the cows like the local Wave Radio, apparently. While I was there they were calving too, and the children were always asking the owners – cool brother and sister Tom and Kimmie, who are the sort of people you would like to have been in your 20s – when the eagerly awaited calves would appear.

The lodges are canvas- and wood-based with excellent quirky features, such as a sink tap coat-hangers and large, beautiful photos of cows – which sounds strange, but it works. There is a very well-equipped kitchen area, two double beds, bunk beds and sitting area with verandah which has its own barbecue and looks out over the fields to the sea.

It is beautiful – notwithstanding the fact that for the three days we were there, it poured with rain. All except for a brief spell one morning, when my son Tom and I learnt to climb a tree with ropes and harness, courtesy of Goodleaf Tree Climbing, the UK's recreational tree climbing specialist. Up the mighty oak we went, ascending to an impressive 50 ft above the ground.

Electric heaters had been placed in the lodges to ward off the unseasonable cold: an un-eco gesture for which Tom – owner, not my son – apologized. Rubbish, I thought: I want to be warm. A wood burning stove was to hand, but there are times when even the most resolute of eco-warriors must take the bigger picture into account.

Toms Eco Lodge is an ideal base for the island's festivals – the Isle of Wight Music Festival in June and the Bestival in September – plus a host of the attractions, such as the Seaview Wildlife Encounter, near Ryde. And Wight is an easy island to see by car although the eco-bridged would doubtless get about by bike.

All in all, a warm welcome to the eco-realm. Rice cakes with cream on, as it were.

F

Firsts

The first time you see a whale. The first time you sky dive from a plane, the first time you see New Zealand, the first time you fly into Hong Kong and out of it. Never forget the first.

G

Guides

One of the best plays I've ever seen starred Margaret Tyzack and the wonderful Dame Maggie Smith. Lettice and Lovage concerns a woman (Lettice Douffet, aka Damie Maggie) who is hired to show tours round an old stately home and who, in her desire to attract more customers – and to prevent herself from dying of boredom – begins to fabricate tales of ghosts and murders in the house.

The crowds and takings grow in direct proportion to Lettice's lies. In the end, her fabulous frolic results in summary dismissal, yet what struck me most was the wonderous power of storytelling, and how a tour guide's delivery is as important as anything he or she might say.

Over the years, I have been privileged to meet some excellent guides during the course of my travels. Not only do they know their stuff, but on the rare occasions when they don't they are honest enough to admit it – and dedicated enough to find the answer pretty fast. They understand their audience and use pathos, wit and even shock tactics to enhance their performance (for that's exactly what it is). Best of all are those who are indigenous to the region and passionate about their subject, but who also retain a sense of humour.

Like the redoubtable Mr Yip – quite probably the oldest tour guide on the planet – on the Malaysian paradise island of Pangkor Laut. At 92, he still leads groups of up to 20 into the island rainforest, where by now he must know just about every single creature, probably by name. His speciality is spelling out in gruesome, technicolour detail what would happen if one were bitten by this snake, or that spider, and how quickly and painfully death would ensure. That sort of stuff you remember.

Working in radio, I've always been deeply aware of the power of words and the importance of using them to paint pictures in the mind. So are all the best tour guides. Words add another dimension, like transforming a photo into a painting, adding something original to encourage listeners to view the scene in a deeper way.

Pathos is an important part of this. In Skagway, Alaska, which formed a base for prospective miners during the 1890s Yukon gold rush, there are guides who recite the poetry of Robert Service. The 'Canadian Kipling', as he was known, was actually a Scot who came to the area and fell in love with it, and his poetry is as haunting as it is accurate in its description of a region both beautiful and harsh. The guides are actors who take on the role of Service himself, and there's never a dry eye at the end.

Not that being a tour guide is a fast route to easy applause. Lack of proper preparation can be lethal, as I can testify from personal experience. After school I worked in Italy with a tour operator, which organised trips around the prettiest parts of the world, on foot or by bike. None of the walks I was supposed to lead were signposted and I felt a bit like an explorer, trying to remember which path I should cross, and at which unremarkable tree I should turn. I was allowed one rehearsal with a guide who did everything at breakneck speed. If we'd had digital cameras in those days I would have taped the route. Alas, we did not.

So along with a girl called Eliana – two years older than me and far more sensible – off I went into the Ligurian unknown. The two of us had a group of 10 – 12 to show round – and hopefully, bring safely back from – the stunning coastal villages of the Cinque Terre.

The result? Well, lets just say that my initial effort yielded precious few tips. I got my group lost twice during that first, turbulent week, turning left at the wrong road and right at the wrong pine. Not easy, trees.

But I learned. On my second tour, not only did I keep the group firmly on track, but I also saw them safely through a raging forest fire. The tips were better.

My grasp of the area was limited, but I made the most of what knowledge I had. I didn't do a Maggie Smith on them, but hopefully I did inject some passion and provide them with some memorable experiences – even if they weren't always as listed on their itinerary. Eliana was excellent and organised and, in many ways, not unlike the Margaret Tyzack character, keeping us both on the straight and narrow. By and large we had as much of a holiday as the guests did.

Twenty years on, I am still in contact with Eliana and some of the guests, so it can't have been all bad. But then, that's the beauty of tours. The words and images of the best guides remain with you for a lifetime. And sometimes, if you're lucky, so do the guides.

H

Habitual, habit forming

Despite the holiday programmes, the wonderful books on the incredible exploits of adventurers, of the verbose and prosaic descriptions of aspirational if not inspirational travel in the national broadsheets, most of us (over 75%) go to the same part of Spain every year for sun, sand and sea, egg and chips. Habit or lack of imagination? Neither – laziness.

Hotels

Hotels are an irrelevance when travelling. They are what matters when on holiday. They can tell you a little about the culture but they provide somewhere that has the semblance of safety and 'what you know'. Nothing more. They are not part of the adventure. Don't treat them that way. They have been adapted to integrate you into the culture so that you feel safe should you want to retreat somewhere. If you stay in a hotel compound for the duration of your stay, you haven't seen the country.

I

iPhones, iPads, i-anything (technology)

In some ways technological progress has greatly enhanced the holiday experience. In particular, the Internet enables us rapidly to compare and contrast the cost, value and times of particular trips; information which, in the past, would have generally required hours to unearth, waiting to speak to a travel agent who may well have known her product, but not how to adapt it to individual needs.

Thanks to the web, we now have the facility to mix and match. Furthermore, we can do it from our own home, in our own time. Many hotels and destinations are now producing taster videos, giving a sense of what you can expect for your money.

Technology allows us to make real journeys in the blink of an eye, when once they would have taken for ever. In the diabolical days of the Atlantic slave trade, the voyage from Africa to the Americas could last months: now the trip is just seven hours by plane. Everywhere is accessible, with the possible exception of the Moon. And even that's not far off thanks to Mr Branson.

All the technology in the world will not, thankfully make redundant certain functions of the will. Think again of those proliferating websites and reflect upon the fact that, even when we have researched ourselves silly, we still need to make a choice. Technology widens our options, but the power of decision remains with us. Indeed, the sheer volume of information can act as more of a hindrance than a help, submerging us beneath the waves of spurious fact. Spoilt for choice we may be, but there are those who would insist that we have been spoilt *by* choice as well.

Note too that website information is only as good as those who input it. Errors – deliberate or otherwise – do occur, especially as the people behind the site are essentially there to sell you a holiday, not to improve your chances on Mastermind. I recently stayed at a hotel which looked nothing whatsoever like the pictures on its website. Eventually it dawned on me that the palatial looking rooms were actually from another hotel in the group – a hotel for which I'm still looking.

But remember, journeys are much like food: fast doesn't necessarily mean good. Accelerated trips are in danger of killing off the art of travel. Take away all of the struggle; edit out the hours of gently rising expectations; lose the joy of drifting at a leisurely pace, eyes wide open to each passing delight; do all this and much of the romance goes too.

In short, there are times when one needs to be utterly cut off, distanced spiritually, geographically and even technologically from home. Leave the iPhones and iPads at home.

J

Joneses – as in keeping up with them

The media tell us we are inadequate if we don't go to the places, see the things, or do the things that the celebrities or adventurous do.

I remember a journalist in the *Times* writing, of HAVE TODDLER WILL TRAVEL that I was unadventurous not mentioning enough about travel to South America. Over 70% of the population of the UK didn't leave the UK for France, let alone Ecuador.

Like fashion, travel has trends, all of which should be politely ignored.

What is good for your neighbour isn't good for you, only for a cycle of one up manship that transcends all reason and budget. Celebrities rarely pay for their own holidays, tans and accommodation, so ignore what they do.

Then you have the 'famous' travellers. The Brysons, Palin, Attenborough, all well-known for their expertise. Watch them. They are entertaining and informative and informed. Adapt what they tell you to your own needs. Do not copy them verbatim. They are there as 'guides' not as gurus.

And travel brochures paint the pictures of places, as though we are inadequate if we don't go to this hotel, visit that city, sky dive from that plane. It's nonsense, of course. Travel doesn't automatically make you a more insightful person. There are those who travel the world, meet the indigenous tribes of outer Mongolia, and return still as lacking in compassion and insight as when they left.

Journeys

Life is a series of them. Think of life that way, and you will appreciate how much you achieve every day.

K

K-Pax

Go watch this film again and again and again. There is a line in it which is significant. Kevin Spacey at the end says 'you will travel on this same journey and make the same mistakes over and over and over again until you get it right.' So start to take the journeys and think about them differently.

L

Life

Life is a journey. That's what every religion, spiritual self help book, well paid keynote speaker, has said over the twenty years I've been a travel journalist. *It's all about the journey, not about the destination.*

Rubbish. It is about the destination. You wouldn't start out on the journey if you didn't believe, hope, aspire to get somewhere else. You may not reach it, but you aim to get there at some stage. And life is about living it to the full potential, surviving, enjoying, thriving, until you get to the end either with a bang, unexpected full stop or a slow exit from the stage.

Luxury

Luxury is relative. One person's luxury is another's run-of-the-mill. Luxury is sold to you as the best seat in the house, the best of everything. But wanting the best, the luxurious, has a perverse effect on the experience of travel. Buying into luxury makes you stick to the seat you are in, because you've paid so much for it. It immobilises you, rather than sets you free. Think about it.

M

Misery

If only one could fly. Just think of all the airport horrors it would save. Terminals, schedules, extortionate parking charges, wickedly seductive retail outlets and traffic systems that were clearly designed to aggravate the customer. Forget *Airport Live – Come Fly with Me* gets closer to the truth than any buzzings from a fly on the wall. Lord knows how Edward Snowden managed to sustain sanity in the airport for so long.

So when an invitation arrived to spend a whole day in one of these outposts of Hades – albeit one with a string of awards to mark it as the best in Europe – I was surprised to hear myself accept. It's not in the UK, of course – it's Schiphol, Amsterdam. The most environmentally friendly airport in the world, apparently, despite the fact that it boasts six runways and over 51 million passengers a year. And prolific sales of tulips and clogs.

Now you can see for yourself. For the modest sum of 15 euros (7.50 for children) Schiphol is running behind the scenes, multimedia guided tours: fire station, snow fleet, airplane hangars and all. For plane-spotters and under 9s, it's the birthday present of a lifetime.

Always assuming that you can get there: which, in my case, was looking a dodgy bet when I found myself lost in the lift at Heathrow, searching vainly for the sign to departures. But a 45 minute flight saw me touch down safely in the Shangri-La of Schiphol, which specialises in transfers to long haul destinations. I've been there in transit myself, and though there are other places where I would rather spend my last day on Earth, it certainly comes up to scratch.

But what exactly makes it the best? Well for a start there is loads of space and light that compares favourably to say, Stansted. Families are well catered for too, even though most of Schiphol's business is business. There are good play areas, while the babycare room reminds me of an upmarket romantic restaurant, of the kind in which the tables are set behind semi-transparent silk curtains. Odd, isn't it, that the airports with the best child facilities always seem to be the ones that need them the least?

There's a large lounge area with a big screen and comfortable reclining chairs. It reminds me of the movie *Soylent Green*, set in the future, in which people just before they die go to a room with tinky-tinky music and a screen showing beautiful scenes. Not so great, perhaps, if you've seen that particular film and are about to board a plane.

Then there's a casino, complete with clock and sign indicating departures, ensure that you won't lose track of time – even if you lose al your money. There are several hotels, including one in which rooms must be booked for at least four hours. And the KLM Crown Lounge has a deep sleep area consisting of about 20 cubicles, each with a smile reclining couch set in near darkness. Abandon hope of catching your flight, all ye who enter here without an alarm.

Signs around the airport point to bars, restaurants and McDonald's as though the latter were some utterly distinct alternative to mainstream catering – which I suppose it is. Certainly the man-sized McDonald's clown sitting on alone on the benches looks more sinister than welcoming. Perhaps he's annoyed that Schiphol is committed to healthy eating with more sushi and salad and juice bars than fast food.

Other curiosities include a panoramic terrace with a Fokker 100, which looks as though it had missed the runway and decided to take up residence on the roof. A library where you can download books onto your iPhone; and a grand piano which anyone can play. There is even a nod towards the great, defining landmarks of life, in the form of a mortuary and – should the fancy come upon you – a place to get married.

More practically, self-service check in areas make life much easier, along with machines enabling you to check in your own luggage. These look like relics from *Star Trek*, but Schiphol is very proud of them.

Best of all, however are the XpresSpa area, where stress and tension relief are just a heart beat away. Waiting times are no more than 10 minutes, but you are usually seen on demand. It's the ideal facility for airports – much better than butchering the Moonlight

Sonata on a grand piano or blowing your inheritance at roulette.

Still, enough was enough. Award winning it may be, but after a whole day at Schiphol, I just wanted to fly home. And therein lies the irony. It can be as luxurious as you like, but the success of an airport is ultimately measured by how efficiently it gets you through. Once you are safely in the air, not even the best in Europe can excite a backward glance.

N

No

No travel book, however evocatively written, nor any skilfully edited TV show can provide a substitute for firsthand impressions. In the end, both consist of highly subjective comments by someone you don't know, and with whom you probably have nothing in common. To settle for such pale shadows is self-robbery. They're nothing more than guides – and just because you have the guide, it doesn't mean that you've finished or even started the journey.

P

Perfume counter

This is the nick-name given to those who work in travel journalism – writers, reporters, bloggers, reviewers, brochure writers, broadcasters. Anyone who has walked slowly down a beach and looked into the camera lens and announced 'The people here are so friendly'.

Perfume Counter journalists make everything look, sound, feel, and appear much better than it is. Unlike the rest of journalism, which (if not all the time) tends to point out the negative.

In twenty years in the travel industry, working as a travel journalist, author , broadcaster, and – when the magazines will take them – photographer, I've noticed how newspapers and magazines write up travel reports. How some newspapers ban certain phrases and words, (nice, worldly, stunning views, incredible landscape, melting pots), and how they still get in. Advertising revenue perhaps dictates when the article isn't sweet smelling enough.

I tended to get round this by writing what the editor wanted, and then writing a novel – fictional of course – about characters traveling and the reality of the situation. One book: SCHOOL'S OUT – YOU DON'T KNOW WHO YOUR FRIENDS ARE UNTIL YOU GO ON HOLIDAY WITH THEM, has more truth in it about certain destinations than you will find in any guidebook, brochure or blog. To publish it, I had to call it fiction – so watch out for travel journalists turning novelists. That's where you'll find the interesting stuff.

Of course, thanks to social media, and review sites such as Tripadvisor, everyone is a travel writer, and they aren't so complimentary. This doesn't mean they are right – just right by their own perception, their definition of what good (or bad) looks like.

Plato

According to the philosopher Plato, no one should travel to merge with other cultures until they reached the age of forty. His view was not based on the premise that life begins at forty or on mid life crisis hitting, but more to do with minimizing the indiscriminate merging of cultures which he argued would bring out the worst rather than the best in the individual. Furthermore, he suggested, travelers should be restricted to the ports of cities to avoid contact with 'native citizens'. Plato would have approved of 'cruising' as a holiday option.

Plato based this intriguing view on 'acculturation' which – without getting too psycho-babble – explains the process of cultural and psychological change that occurs when two cultures meet.

Plato felt there were positives and negatives to cultures merging and that in general the negative outweighed the positive. This is an argument which appears as pertinent now as it did in the times of Plato. However for the purpose of this book I'm focusing on the positive emotional impact of a journey rather than the political, social and economic implications of mass migration.

Platitudes

Everyone learns about themselves from their journeys. Wrong. Just as wealthy travellers spends tens of thousands travelling to far flung destinations and can only recount at the dinner table how much everything cost, many travel but very few actually learn about the places they visit – let alone about themselves. They don't even learn that they don't learn. In fact, the ones who learn are the ones who live with, or know, the ones who don't learn. The people who go to counselling are the ones who want to learn. The ones who don't, feel they know it already.

It's not about the destination. Well, to say life is not about the destination is saying sex is great without the orgasm, or studying for the exam is enough without taking and passing it. That's rubbish. The destination is the focus, it may change along the way as the result of the journey, but it is necessary to point you in a direction, any direction, wrong or right, just a direction. And stop you from being static, isolated, alone.

Perception

When you're this old you can reconsider your whole life. You can relive your life and understand it with a pleasure and perception not available when you first experienced it.
Polly Kline, aged 101

Read that quote by Polly Kline again. 'A pleasure and perception not available when you first experienced it'. There's that word 'perception' again, which the Professor mentions a lot. Arguments are caused not because we fundamentally disagree about something, but because we see something from different perspectives. That sounds the same, but isn't. That's why traveling by RV through the Rockies of Canada left a family on BBC's programme 'Perfect Holiday' yawning with boredom despite a group of 'travel experts' suggesting this would be the perfect travel experience for them. Nope. So who was right? The family were. Their perception, their truth, their thoughts and feelings.

Did they regret not making the most of their trip to Canada? "I don't need a trip to Canada," the dad told me later (I wasn't one of the experts by the way). "I need a break with the kids on a beach in the South of France, camping. That's what I need. It works for me." So it's not a case of right or wrong, it's a case of perception and definition.

Of course, looking back on travels, even after you have finished your journey, you will reflect and see so much more than when you first experienced it. It's like looking at a diamond and asking its worth, and then seeing the rainbow light it creates around itself when you move it, how looking deeply it can transfix you, almost hypnotise you. You realize the value you put on it is totally different from that just offered. Or not. Perhaps the dad in ten years time will need that trip to Canada, with his wife or grown-up kids. But at the moment, that's not what he needs. Or wants.

Poetry

If you are inspired to write a poem about your trip, it's meant something, even if you can't write poetry. It's the inspiration that counts, and it always leads to something else. Like one of Professor de Bono's thinking games, it's a way to notice and reflect on the diamond of the travel experience and enjoy the impact it has on your feelings and thoughts. For example, my trip on an African safari ten years ago made me think differently about the safari experience– something I'd thought I already understood.

AFRICAN SAFARI

The heartbeat of life echoes in the darkness
As primal dancers taste the air
Their rainbow of raw passion fails to move
Still white men colour-blind to the nature of the beast
Who have no sense
And no sense of what they see
Holding their breath and closing their heart
To the seduction and wisdom of the moment
In case they might feel the tightening chains of their own
making
Africa is a place more evolving and deep and immense
Than they bear to believe exists outside their boxed little
world
And expired imagination
They click impatiently through a tiny camera lens
Seeing nothing
But a tick on the dinner party 'have dones' before the port
and wine

Are wasted
Destroying everything they approach by admiring too closely
Below and above the ground.
The lions sleep and cheetah yawn unable to camouflage how
Weary and bored and disinterested they are at our ignorant curiosity
These pussy-cats always keep one eye open, waiting for us to make the fatal mistake that they are our friends
Hoping one day they will get the chance to eat us alive as we are now devouring them
But less humanely
I absorb and breathe in the pain and anger and wonder
As I skim through by train and car and foot this place
And cry and laugh inside by turn
At the violent magnificent contrast of mountain and plain
And rumbling discontent
Of a land that screams out to deaf ears to be left alone
And I sense again that primal rhythm I heard on my first day
As I watched the dancers
And I start to move to a beat I find infectious
And overwhelmingly humbling
Of a proud people far smarter than our own
Still treated despite the Lighthouse Man
Like cute animals allowed to live like organ grinders
To perform for greedy men
Who don't tolerate any rhythm that isn't their own
Not realising it's not theirs at all
Every single living thing in this vital and raw and important land
Dances to the rhythm of Original Life
A rhythm I know, until I came here I had almost forgotten

And only to its echo my Game Boy son may one day learn to dance.

Q

Questions

Ask questions of yourself before you go. You'll learn a lot about yourself and what makes you tick when travelling.

On my travel show on Jazz Fm, I always asked celebrities who they would most like to travel with on long journeys in an RV. Someone interesting, someone handsome or beautiful, someone hilarious and a good cook always made the grade.

I would take my son, who is a good traveller, my late father – because I would like him to spend time with his grandson – President Nixon, Gandhi, and the Professor. I just realised I'm the only woman, not one of them is a cook, and no one is young and handsome (as in Brad Pitt handsome). Says a lot about why I travel then. Who would you choose? And why?

Also, which language would you most like to speak fluently if you could? And why?

Where would you like your ashes scattered?

Where do you have absolutely no interest in going?

What's the most horrific experience you've had whilst travelling?

Ask these questions of yourself and write them down. You have the start of a story and a journey.

Questionnaires

The good companies will acknowledge and act upon them. Most of those in the travel industry take little heed of what you say. If you have a complaint or comment say it at the time, say it after the time, but don't tick-box a form – ever.

R

Repetition

Every year over a million of us return to the resort we visited the summer before. Travel writers may wax lyrical about the lure of unfamiliar destinations, but when it comes to holidays, the majority of Brits seem determined to play it safe.

And there's nothing wrong with that. Annual leave is a precious commodity – squander it, and the chances are that you'll be waiting 12 more months for a shot at heaven on earth.

But for some British holidaymakers – around 100,000 each year – the retro pull extends further than the previous summer. These are the ones who, drawn by a potent mix of curiosity and nostalgia, elect to return to their childhood holiday haunts, travelling hopefully back to the land of lost content.

The idea has a powerful appeal. Yet in reality, paradise can be maddeningly hard to regain. The coasts of Europe, for example, have fallen prey to the snare of overdevelopment, and many resorts once full of charm are merging slowly into the concrete jungle. At disturbingly frequent intervals along the Med, memory lane has turned into the highway to hell.

Recently after gaps of 30 years, two colleagues of mine each made a pilgrimage to their respective pasts. One travelled to the central Algarve, in Portugal, the other to the east coast of Spain. Both returned horribly depressed.

The first was horrified at the maze of the kiss-me-quick English breakfast banners, the proliferation of flat vowels and bad architecture, and the mass of blubbery burnt skin packed onto beaches that were a shadow of their former selves. Gone were the quaint and mildly eccentric owners, replaced by skyscrapers that seared the soul. And the little restaurants that once offered menus using only local produce, simply prepared with no concessions to foreign tastes, have evolved into ghetto-blasting bars with everything from pole dancers to 24-hour Sky TV. A travel writer herself, my colleague wondered ruefully if her words of praise had helped to kill the place she had so admired all those years ago.

My second acquaintance returned to a resort which, on the face of it, had actually gone upmarket. In her eyes, however it had deteriorated into an equally soulless sham. Here the City boys and their families – the only ones who could afford the inflated prices – thronged the array of charmless hotels and restaurants, showering their brand of emptiness upon a place where money screamed.

For my colleague, it was a painfully metaphorical jolt. Once in that vanished childhood when she was last here, she had dreamed of being a dancer, an actress and artist. Now she herself worked in the City. Like the haven of her youth, she had sold out to the silver dollar.

Of course, it doesn't have to be like that. Retracing childhood steps can help to foster the realisation of how far one has come in life – not just materially, but spiritually and emotionally too.

Such feelings were my experience upon my return to Emilia Romagna, the prosperous region of Italy where I spent many happy holidays as a child. Here, in the breadbasket of the old Roman Empire, lived some of the greatest cultural talents of the 20th Century – Pavarotti, Toscanini and Verdi, to name but three. Here too you will find the best Italian food: Pecorino and ricotta cheeses, prosciutto and Parma hams, balsamic vinegar, prugnolo wild mushrooms, Romagnola beef, civitella cherries, and white truffles.

For seven years, from the ages of 9 – 18, I visited this place. My father would drive our car mercilessly south, pounding the autoroutes and autostrasse and pausing only for the odd double espresso, until finally we reached the seaside town of Cesenatico, perched neatly behind its brasher neighbour Rimini. Here we would pitch tent in a campsite five minutes walk from the beach.

A quarter of a century later, Cesenatico had lost none of its charm. Nor had Forli, the architecturally refined town where they sold the best ice cream and where the ornate square was ideal for chase and tag. This time round, I took my nine-year-old son to play the same games with his forty-something mother.

Revisiting the past reinforced my positive feelings about the present. I reflected that, although life's journey had sometimes been rocky – not unlike those long drives down to the campsite – I was where I wished to be.

At nine, somewhere implausibly, I had wanted to be an angel. I figured that I'd be able to travel the world for free, landing whenever and wherever I wanted, pouring happiness or disdain upon those I loved or loathed. Today I'm certainly no angel, but looking back at my childlike criteria, I suppose that being a travel writer comes close.

S

Sabbatical

Duncan Goose, CEO of One Brand, took a two-year trip round the world on a motorbike six years ago as a sabbatical from his high powered job in advertising; not because he likes travelling, but because he likes motor bikes. He experienced hurricanes – the second worst one in the history of the world (Hurricane Mitch in Honduras), was shot at by bandits in Mexico, and nearly fell off a narrow dust road in the Andes. He thought he was going to die at the Afghan border, but it wasn't any of these 'big' stories on his journey that made him start One Brand.

After Hurricane Mitch there was devastation. Houses were submerged in mud. There was nothing. There was nothing to dig the houses out with so everyone just stood and stared. No one tried. But he found a roof tile. He started to dig. Then others joined in and found other roof tiles. They dug. And they dug the house out of the mud. And then another, just using roof tiles. One person can do a lot of good. One tile made a difference. One journey makes a difference.

Did he intend this round-the-world motorbike trip to be seminal? No. He wanted two years off from his job in advertising. He wasn't going for an 'Eat, Pray, love' epiphany.

Just as in the book *The Alchemist*, or , you rarely discover at the end of the journey what you went out to seek. Gold, knowledge, self or otherwise, is shown to you in ways you are unable to imagine or hope for. But you've got to take that first step. And it's a step best taken alone, as Duncan did, and I did in Malta when I met the Professor. You have to talk to people.

Stupid

The late Sir Magnus Magnusson told me 'In Iceland the word for 'stupid' translates as 'person who does not travel." They stagnate. It is nothing to do with seeing the world, meeting new people, learning new languages, or improving your skiing. It's to do with making the most of yourself. We briefly recognize that as teenagers, and then we forget.

Souvenirs

I have a passion for rings. In fact, I'm fast running out of fingers on which to wear them. The present count is nine – rings that is, not fingers.

It all started in Canada during a visit to Halifax, Nova Scotia, when I wandered into a craft fair at which a woman was selling beaded rings in a variety of colours. I bought one. Now I have rings from all around the globe. India, Prague, France, Italy, USA: not even darkest Chiswick has escaped my reach. It's a kind of motivation tool : each time I have a book published, a beautiful ring is my reward.

Of course, swanning around town like an outcrop of Hatton Garden has its price. Again and again I am asked to tell the story behind each ring – where I bought, why I bought, from whom I bought from and so on. But I don't mind. My collection is a pleasant reminder of my diverse travels, like an indelible photo in the mind that instantly flashes up each time I look at my hands.

Rarely, however, do I feel the need to go on a journey to purchase something just for the sake of it. Ring addiction aside – along with a penchant for First Nation Canadian sculpture – I'm not a great one for souvenirs. They have an in-built tendency to disappoint, frequently catching the eye in their natural habitat while failing to look the part back home. No matter how boho you think you are,

Richmond Hill does a pale imitation of deepest Rajasthan.

Of course, some mementoes are actually very practical. I always travel light, buying my T-shirts on location, and these double up as souvenirs. Mind you, I draw the line at the 'I've been to Hayling Island' variety, as I know how I react to other people wearing such stuff. The word 'part' comes effortlessly to mind.

This is probably why I find souvenir shops at airports, hotels resorts and so on a complete waste of space, designed for those benighted folk whom nature has failed to bestow with imagination. What sort of being, pray, invests in 'Our Mother' ear muffs at Lourdes, or that disgusting durian fruit at Bangkok airport? Apparently, one can even buy the latter in crisp form.

As it happens, my son chooses the best souvenirs in the world. He has a thing for snow globes, but we've had so many of the bloomin' things confiscated from our hand luggage at customs, they're liquid after all – that I try to keep him away from that counter. In any case, a polished, odd shaped pebble rescued from a Cornish beach has far greater meaning than a much-reproduced painting of a view that's tired before you've handed over the credit card.

When he was five, my son wrote a diary of his first safari. Badly spelt and painful to write – for it was his heartless mother who made him bash it out on location – it is still the best souvenir of any journey I've ever shared with him. With its photos, its drawings of elephants that look more like lions, and its short, spiky sentences rejoicing in the lions' indolent delight – well, ok, he didn't quite put it like that – it was a classic of the genre. Much better (and cheaper) than a stuffed fluffy tiger toy, of a kind that I could easily have bought at Hamleys.

Back in the adult world, one of my most unusual and inspired souvenirs came from a recent trip to California. Here I visited the Ojai Spa Resort, set in a stunning part of the state, 15 miles inland and a good 10 degrees hotter than LA. You can learn to surf, ride, play golf and generally do a multitude of things – or not, as the mood dictates – while the spa has a wide range of signature treatments designed to relax, detox and invigorate you, though preferably not all at the same time. Here too is the most enchanting, inspired and original concept I've encountered in a very long time – the apothecary's cottage.

This place offers an art programme which includes silverpoint drawing and silk scarf painting, as well as the change to create and christen your own personal scent of essential therapeutic oils. I called my heady mix of orange and ylang ylang Oomph – which is exactly what my stay at the Ojai Spa gave me. One can also create a 'mandala' a cosmic diagram reminding us of our relation to the infinite, for interpretation by the amazing Rea, who I think is a white witch – albeit a lovely ne. Needless to say, my own drawing revealed me to be extremely creative (lots of orange, blues and reds) in touch with my subconscious (plenty of black long-legged spiders) and possessing a dark side (red mountains pointing

upwards, as mountains of all colours generally do).
Mind you, my ex-husband could have told you that
bit without the drawing.

Whatever it says, it's a unique souvenir of a
unique and soulful resort, literally leaving you will
the essence of the place and your time there. I shall
return to Ojai for more sunshine and oompth. As for
the ear-muffs and crassly sloganed T shirts, it's a case
of goodbye to all tat.

Soul-searching

When I was a child, all I wanted from my holiday was
a campsite on a beach, and I was happy. When I was
a teenager, I want to be with kids my own age, to look
cool. In my twenties, I wanted a holiday tan in two
weeks that looked like I'd been there for two months,
and then wanted to achieve and improve myself,
through kick-boxing or adventures, or anything far
flung or dangerous sounding. And in my thirties I
started to write about my experiences, so my travels
became almost surreally third-party as I spent my
travel time noting detail, accent and culture – things I
wouldn't do if I was genuinely on holiday.

Now I've reached my forties, I'm travelling with
my son who finds everything new and wonderful,
and as a result I find myself seeking out destinations
that give me a greater sense of inner well-being. I'm
not talking spa pampering here, or holistic yoga, or
pilates holidays. Pampering the body isn't enough
any more. The latest trend when travelling is to
pamper the soul, to take an internal journey as well as

an external one, and to seek out journeys or destinations that offer what you might call a special energy.

For some time, celebrities have been making well publicised visits to meet spiritual figures like the Dalai Llama, but everyone has access to destinations offering more than merely material comforts. Some are obvious, such as Jerusalem and Stonehenge, others less obvious like Utah, Bruges, and the Tarn and Garonne regions of France. These places offer a chance of self-improvement that reaches deeper than the external pampering of the health spa, or merely eating what the locals eat.

T

Trends

Like fashion they come and go, and may not suit your budget or your mood. Don't follow them – you'll end up paying more, and feel manipulated into doing something you only realise when you've returned home.

U

Unique

All journeys are unique in one way: you're the one doing it. Your perception is totally unique to you. Be aware of being told what to think, or how you should think about something you see, taste, or do.

Up

Mountains. Up, up, up, and away. Go up in the world if you want to literally and metaphorically raise your spirit. Cleaner air, more space, fresh breath. Up, go up. Not by the sea. UP! Got that? Any mountain will do. Kilimanjaro, skiing in the Alps, even Everest – or, as I suggest, below the Base Camp because you'll meet the Sherpas who keep their feet on the floor despite going up to the highest mountain in the world. Something some of those they guide fail to do.

V

Vox pop

Always beware of vox pop results where opinion on destinations is concerned. A thousand people in Camden will tell you different from a thousand in Pimlico and they're only a few miles a part. How people respond is all dependent on so many factors – when they were asked; the time of day; the weather; if they've had an argument with their partner; or just come back or going on holiday. Just because 1000 people say they prefer Spain to Italy doesn't mean they're right or you need to.

I asked 1,000,000 of us in the UK over the past seven years (the internet is an amazing thing) about why we travel. I asked them one question. Why do you travel? They had to answer in no more than fifteen words. This was their response.

holiday
business
to see relations
to see friends
to discover new places
to learn something new
to chill
to escape
to 'tick box' a destination (ie say you've been there)
something to do

What an unimaginative bunch we are! I wasn't expecting 'to make the world a better place,' or 'to find enlightenment,' or 'because I want to find out who I am' or 'because I'm curious about the world around me and don't want to wake up sixty and feel like Shirley Valentine and that I've lived a very small life,' but the open questions elicited answers that either revealed a desperation for the next break or something to be endured – especially if they had a family in tow – their words, not mine. It's not as if life has no meaning without traveling. That would be like saying life has no meaning if you don't have a baby. It's a matter of perspective, after all. But in a world that is continually seeking for ways to feel 'better, stronger, fitter, happier', travel, the right type of travel, provides a source of counseling which doesn't require sitting in a counselor's chair, saying Ommmm cross-legged in a studio, dating someone half your age to show you are half your age, and throwing the baby out with the bathwater because a big change is as good as a big rest.

We may go on holiday and return reinvigorated, but it lasts a short time. We also go on holiday and may return less invigorated than when we left. So is this to do with bad choice of destination, or something more intrinsic to our psychology?

No wonder the world seems smaller when there is so little imagination put into the reasons behind why we travel, when the seeing and doing of travel is we feel all there is to it.

Vanishing Points

I've just received a report commissioned by Churchill Travel Insurance (never heard of it) on the subject of 'disappearing destinations'. By which it means places destined to burn out and turn into desert (much of Africa) sink and become sea (Venice, San Francisco, Vancouver) or fall victim to cultural destruction (anywhere in Europe and Asia visited by bonus-brained bankers). Never mind the earthquakes, there's nothing like a tourist eruption to shake the foundations of the past.

Now reports are what all insurance companies go in for when they want to make you fearful of doing or not doing something. Consequently, they tend to end up in my bin. This one, however, attracted my attention, as it touched upon a recurring theme of my time as a travel writer. Many are the sombre press releases I have received, informing me that I 'must' – absolutely must – visit a particular destination before it goes. Apocalypse tomorrow – opportunity now.

But you know what? Even taking account of the very real threat from global warming, I'm not absolutely convinced. Especially after my trip to the Maldives. This low lying island group is definitely a prime contender in the soon to be submerged stakes, and when I visited 10 years ago, the guide told me candidly that the island I was on would soon be no more than a memory. Yet a decade later not a single grain of sand looked out of place.

Not that the scare stories are entirely without foundation. In North America, for example, the subtropical swamps and marshes of the Everglades in Florida are very much at risk from hurricanes, while the fascinating cities of Vancouver and San Francisco both lie on the ticking time bomb of a fault line. Meanwhile the Great Barrier Reef in Australia, one of the largest marine ecosystems in the world, is in danger from the ever-increasing volume of cruise ships. A neat irony, really as the burgeoning fleet is partly down to the tourist boards urging punters to se the reef before it goes – rather like getting people to drive 200 miles to buy petrol.

Yet whenever I've spoken to local experts on my travels, they have always been very philosophical about the places they love. Nature, they say, always finds a way to fight back. Even such devastations as the Australian forest fires – unspeakable tragedies tough they are – sever ultimately to give the landscape a fresh start: to enable nature to renew itself and flourish again.

True, the prognosis isn't always so bright. In Italy, for instance, the Amalfie Coast and Tuscany are both in line for an increase in heatwaves, with hot and humid nights and a heightened risk of fire. The same goes of Turkey and Greece, where the heat already approaches furnace levels during July and August. But these places have their cool, wet winters, when the visitors retreats and the landscape can breathe again. Reports of the demise of such glorious destinations would appear to be somewhere premature.

Perhaps in the end, the real threat is not so much to the landscapes themselves, but to the diversity of culture around the globe. If you really must press the panic button, visit Cuba before it changes out of all recognition. Visit the unspoilt waters and medieval towns of Croatia, before tourism dilutes their distinctive appeal. Visit northern India and Kathmandu Valley of Nepal where the Himalayan ski market is taking off and likely to destroy the local architecture in its wake.

If only it were the miserable and inane places that were in danger. Built on sand, greed and money, Dubai is a synthetic affront to good taste where the only thing to admire is Emirates – the airline out. Nature may abhor a vacuum, but if this place were to vanish, the desert itself would rejoice.

W

Womans World

Lone female adventurers are nothing new. Mary Kingsley, the Victorian explorer, fended off a crocodile in Africa with the paddle of her canoe, and then later fell in a pit of sharp stakes, saved from death by the thickness of her skirt. Amelia Earheart, the aviation pioneer, perished mid-Pacific while attempting to fly around the world. And Tracy Edwards was a teenage rebel who ran away to the South of France before making her name as a yachtswoman.

In recent years, however, the slightly eccentric image of the female traveller has begun to fade. Instead, it has become common for young middle-class women to journey by themselves, often during a gap year. Typically this amounts to much more than a holiday: helping communities in Africa is a pursuit not limited to Prince Harry.

For older women, reasons for travelling alone range from taking a career break to splitting up with a boyfriend. Then there's divorce. Women are realising that they don't have to rely on a man – they can have a full life without one. With all the social changes that have occurred over the past twenty years, there is little to stop people doing what they want to do.

Even though women have the freedom to move, however, they are frequently constrained by their obligations – such as children. But once their offspring have gone, their sense of adventure emerges again and they are off. This is an excellent thing. These are women who have paid for their children to have a gap year and then thought 'why shouldn't I have that too?'. They have done family holidays, done holidays with their husbands, and now they want something more. The generation of female baby boomers never has any 'me time'.

And it's not the cookery course in Paris, or the art course in Florence, that exerts a magnetic pull. These women are travelling far and wide: to India, the Middle East and beyond to exotic lands full of gracious gentle people – like my personal favourite, Oman. Yet starting out isn't always easy. I remember being afraid the first time I travelled to Tunisia by myself. I couldn't go out at night, nobody spoke English and – as it got dark early – I was stuck in a ghastly hotel room with no windows for 12 hours. People didn't smile at me; there was no tourist culture; it was tough.

But then I did an amazing trip to Marrakesh in Morocco, walking amongst the souks where there were no other English voices, and suddenly I got it. Being on my own made all the difference. With no companion to bounce things off, I had to confront where I was. Only by myself did I fully engage with the landscape.

I've been on my own – or with just my young son – on all my best trips. It's made me braver and more creative. Alone in India, North Africa and the

Middle East, facing up to the challenges, I was able to clarity my purpose and direction. It made me realise that I wanted to be a novelist. Now I'm on my sixth work of fiction.

Of course, there is stress as well as joy. India, in particular, was a tough trip, due to the hassle I received from men. Sometimes I'd be walking down the street hitting them as I went, while they persistently attempted to grope me.

But the flip side of this is that local women tend to be welcoming. In Tunisia one day I was walking down a street and a woman asked me to have tea with her. We got on well, and after dinner the family asked me if I wanted to stay. I ended up sleeping on the roof of their house for a week. They even took me to a remote village to meet their cousins.

This kind of experience can really make a trip, and is more likely to happen if you are a woman travelling alone. This is especially true when it comes to making friends with local people, as they are likely to e far more wary of inviting a man into their home.

But remember; anywhere can be dangerous. On my travels I would never get into a cab with a dodgy driver late at night. But then, I wouldn't do that in London either. London is one of the most dangerous places I know.

X

Exit and Exes.

You will at some stage return to places you have been with ex-boyfriends or ex-husbands. It will not be the same place and create the same feeling or thoughts in you now. Recognise that and recognise you will feel differently again when you next visit.

Extraordinary trips

To describe a trip as extraordinary, a journey as phenomenal, it must reach deep inside you and change you as a person – the way you think and feel not only about the place and people around you, but about yourself. I have experienced such places. Some are for sharing, others best visited by oneself. They are journeys rather than destinations, and the resonance owed much to the circumstances in which I went. Timing is everything. And frequently it is the simplest and shortest journeys that yield one's 'Rosebud' moments.

Senegal

Sometimes it's the moment that matters; being in the right place at the right time with the right person. Like in Senegal at 8am on a Sunday in a church in the middle of a desert, listening to Gregorian chants sung by African monks while others played musical instruments. Or listening to a guide, that same weekend, shout emotionally about the treatment of

African slaves before their passage to the Americas, before they left the stunning Ile de Gorée; and about how everyone bewails the Holocaust while ignoring the hundreds of thousands that died in the slave trade.

Senegal is an unsung African country with edge – but not the dangerous, full-on razor's edge that characterises so many of its stunning but unstable neighbours. Go and see for yourself.

In Rajasthan on the tiger trail I discovered tigers in the wild, which may not exist in five years time. Such is the greed and corruption that surrounds these precious powerful animals that they will long precede Venice into oblivion. I took my son to seek them out two years ago and was left both angry a the futility of their demise and humbled by their silent magnificence. I am no romantic about animals, but I defy anyone to look into the eyes of a tiger in the wild and not be haunted by their own mortality.

I left not wanting to write about the trip. Ironically, however, it's tourists that keep these animals alive a little longer.

China

In the urban powerhouse that is Shanghai, there were mornings when the tofu-coloured sky sunk so low that it covered any sign of horizon. Industrial evolutions – not least our own – always come at a cost. By 10 am however, the oppression had lifted, while in Beijing the sky was crystal clear throughout the day; a canopy of boundless blue.

Nor was the traffic quite as hellish as I had been led to believe. The Chinese have cleverly invented a system whereby citizens are banned from driving on certain days if a specific number appears in their car registration. There are two banned numbers each day, which keeps traffic down – even if the gains are a trifle uneven. For in China, the number four is considered unlucky, while nine is thought propitious – a fact reflected in the allocation of number-plates. On non-four days, the traffic hardly changes; when nine is banned, the streets are like the Mary Celeste.

Y

Yoga

The world is in midlife crisis. Not just the almost forties and fifties who want a change of job, life or wife, but nature itself. In the past year we've had earthquakes, hurricanes and fires of biblical proportions, like symptoms of some terrible turbulence wracking the heart of Mother Earth.

Hardly surprising, therefore, that retreats are in vogue – though the word somewhat misses the point.

"It's about visiting places that awakens you spiritually, make you confront issues rather than retreat from them," says Stella Photi of Wellbeing Escape (www.wellbeingescapes.com)

"You are not retreating from the world, but confronting it – and yourself – maybe for the first time," agrees life alignment coach Jeff Levin (life-alignment.com). "You are stripping away all life's pointless distractions. It's a big picture journey."

The wilderness of India, for instance, where the key word is 'acceptance', and where living in the moment is made easier by the fact that, for many, mere existence is al there is. It's enough to humble even the shallowest of visitors cocooned in their luxury palaces and air-conditioned coaches.

Or like the mountaintops of Nepal and Bhutan, where the Himalayan currents – to coin a phrase – lift you up where you belong. oOr Ibiza, with its dense and wired energies, or Ojai, California, where hippy is not so much alternative as mainstream.

The area round my own retreat in France, near Najac – where, incidentally, Kate Mosse set her archaeological mystery novel Labyrinth – has an energy all of its own. It was probably stirred up by the Cathars, the dualist sect that challenged the orthodoxies of the Medieval Church and flourished in northern Italy and southern France. That freedom of spirit still endures in those parts, hanging palpably in the air.

Z

Zoo

Animals look best in the wild. That was what struck me when I fist went on safari some 20 years ago and watched them gradually appear – zebra, giraffe, buffalo, lions – at a waterhole in the Addo National park in South Africa. Here, they said, I would be more likely to see an elephant than anywhere else in the world. And I did.

Now, I'm no David Attenborough but there is happiness about animals in the wild which is quite foreign to those in captivity. True, from our human point of view, captive creatures have a certain appeal. One does not generally have to wait long for them to appear – although I did once hang on for almost half an our at London zoo, waiting for some curiously shy polar bears to come out and take their bow, only to be told that they weren't actually there at all. Perhaps there was a moral in the story: convenience should not be the prime consideration when it comes to watching our fellow creatures at play.

Perhaps the best place to see wildlife at its most interesting is the Galapagos, the wondrous, volcanic archipelago in the Pacific to which I recently travelled with my son. Here the giant tortoises and haughty iguana lay side by side with cows and other domestic animals in an utterly incongruous cohabitation. Stunning though they were, the islands were overpopulated with camera-clicking Americans, who splashed around with the turtles and seals and dolphins and sharks in their pursuit of the perfect shot. Yet the animals remained placid, as un-enchanted by us as we were enchanted by them – and not a cage or aquarium in sight.

Of course, there are times when a degree of incarceration works wonders. I have always been dubious of attractions that call themselves 'lands', as if the world, in all its brutal beauty, could be made to conform to some sanitised blueprint of our own. So when I visited a place called Monkey Land in South Africa, I fully expected a Disneyfied destination where one could gawp mindlessly at the monkeys as they amused us with their tricks and imitations of man.

What I actually got was rather different. Our guide became very animated as he led us round, explaining that the place was effectively a wildlife psychiatric ward. The monkeys, formerly pets or the sidekicks of organ grinders, had been abused by their owners not just physically, but mentally too. No longer wild, they required protection from other animals in the nearby forests, as they would otherwise be attacked and killed – more than likely by the baboons. To us they were 'friendly', wanting to be fed, and some rocked from side to side like toddlers in search of comfort in their pain. It made for a distressing scene.

When one of our group remarked upon the cruelty of the baboons, the guide turned on him, his face a sea of flame. The baboons, he said, were doing exactly what they were meant to be doing; it was the animals inside the fence who were sick, and we were the ones who had made them so. I left with the strong impression that our guide had more time for animals than for human beings.

And I agree with him. I never cease to be horrified by the quaint little customs that countries exploit to lure visitors from abroad: bullfighting in Spain, throwing donkeys out of windows in Portugal and – sorry, but I have to say it – foxhunting in our green and pleasant land. Banned it may be, but its spirit refuses to go away. Seal culling in northern Canada may be a necessity, but the degree of brutality involved carries with it the stale odour of relish. And though I'm looking forward to visiting Japan, I loathe its attitude towards animals – especially dolphins. Still, at least the Japanese treat their elderly better than we do.

Often holidays involving animals tread a very fine line between authentic and commercial. And there's nothing wrong with that, provided that line is not crossed. Ranching done properly, with due care for the horses, is a good example of how to get it right. So too is real safari, where you could easily be eaten if you do anything silly. I like that. It's somehow fairer; more respectful of the food chain.

But the best expression of this food chain logic that I've ever encountered was in Canada, when I interviewed a forest ranger in the Yukon. We'd been filming for several weeks and had already seen grizzly bear and moose, kayaked down the Tashanini Rivers and spotted bald eagles. The previous year an English couple out walking had been attacked and eaten by a grizzly. The papers were full of it, and many Canadians feared that the British public would think that grizzlies had a cultivated taste for English blood. The local ranger, however, was unimpressed.

Would it help, I asked him, if there were paths in the parks so that people couldn't get lost? No good, he said: paths would destroy the environment. But they could have saved the lives of those people, couldn't they?

They didn't have to walk in the park – no one asked them to.

But they wanted to see the wildlife, I reasoned. Well, they did, replied the ranger – it ate them. Yes, but, er, it's not exactly good for tourism, is it, if the tourists get eaten?

"The bears were here first" was the ranger's succinct reply.

The bears were here first. I like that answer. Animals may indeed be at their best in the wild. The point is: we aren't.

SEVEN:
CONCLUSION

What you're looking for is not on the other side of the world, it's frequently under your nose. It's just that you have to travel to the other side of the world to realise it. You still have to make the journey. That's what life is all about.
Anon

WHAT HAPPENS WHEN YOU ARRIVE?

Usually, 'where to next'? Or you ponder for a moment and look back at all your Instagram photos which make the places you've been and the people you've met look rosier, more beautiful, more edgy and interesting than they really are. We're all celebrities now, making ourselves look the best we can be – 'like us, but on a good day' as one advert famously says.

Journeys are like rivers, they don't stand still. Actually neither do we, constantly evolving, personalities do not remain static nor do identities, and travel frequently acts as a catalyst to this change

– if it's the right type of journey. This may have something to do with the destination and what you will do when you arrive but its more to do with the type of journey you take and the attitude – and emotional baggage – you take with you.

There is a game where you ask which you prefer – a stream, a lake, a river, or an ocean. I always said an ocean – vast and deep, but now I'm more attracted to rivers – running strong and fast and always leading to bigger things. All the places I am attracted to have a river running through them, or a waterfall pounding down them. Streams are too small, lakes are too still, oceans just lead down. And you have arrived. Of course you haven't, but I like the idea of a river because it makes me feel there is more to come, always something else to be discovered and that you never really 'arrive', you just stop and look around occasionally and then move on: emotionally, physically, spiritually, intellectually.

You gather experiences which you share and help you to grow. I've given examples of journeys that have worked for me – but you will discover something different, because we're all different.

GOALS

Our goals may be different, but when we're heart-broken, we want to mend and learn and not get it broken again. We're the same that way. We all seek inspiration occasionally, we all want to be inspired, we all seek clarity at some point – that's why we take journeys these days. Or why we should. We seek sunshine because it makes us feel good and look good, and when we have good weather in the UK, we stay here – why should we go away?

OBJECTIVES

Before you go travelling, identify what you want to achieve for yourself, emotionally as well as physically.

TASK

How are you going to achieve those objectives? Which steps are you going to take?

EXPLORE/EXPAND

How can you expand or adapt your journey? Are there different paths you can take? Are you flexible, have you allowed flexibility? If not, why not? People travel how they live – so live a little and divert from the beaten track, the chosen one. You will learn more.

CONCLUDE

You will arrive eventually, usually not where you planned, but never where you started. Looking back, you will realise you've evolved into a different person. You've experienced life, lived it big and travelled in your mind, tested your emotions, and broadened your horizons. You will have ticked all the things on your wish list and discovered ten times as many things you never imagined. You could write a book about your journeys. Don't leave it to the likes of Bryson, Palin and Attenborough. You never arrive. You're always learning. Right, Professor?

ABOUT THE AUTHOR

I'm an award winning travel journalist, broadcaster and author of travel books and best selling fictional novelist. I am not passionate about travel. I am passionate *because* I travel. Journeys make me think.

Lightning Source UK Ltd.
Milton Keynes UK
UKOW04f0100310715

256105UK00001B/3/P